Copyright © 2025 Nicola Anne. All rights reserved.

No part of this book may be reproduced, or stored in a retrieval system, or transmitted in any form or by any means, electronic, mechanical, photocopying, recording, or otherwise, without express written permission of the publisher.

ISBN Hardback- 978-1-7644517-0-3
ISBN Paperback- 978-1-7644517-1-0
First published by N.A December 2025.

Nicola Anne is a writer with a background in social sciences, literature, and business, and a permanent curiosity about the way power, culture, and people collide. She has a particular interest in the ethics of the beauty industry, social structures, and the stories we're sold about who we're meant to be.

Feminist, queer, and a mother of two, Nicola balances sharp thinking with real-world grit thanks to her work with families, young people, and vulnerable communities. She writes about identity, relationships, and resilience with humour, heart, and just enough bite.

She's partial to good banter, spirited debate, and the occasional spiced rum.

Thank you to the women who trusted me with their stories. You gave me truth without softening it, and this book is better for it.

Thank you to the men who offered their insights and their stumbling points. Your honesty, your "wait... what?" moments and your occasional defensive detours were far more useful than polished perfection ever could be.
You reminded me that growth isn't tidy, but it is very possible.

This book is for every man who cares about a woman in his life - a mum, a daughter, a sister, a partner, a colleague, a friend.
If you love them, you want the world to treat them better.
If you love them, you want to be someone who makes that easier.

All that takes is a little awareness, curiosity and the willingness to show up a little differently in a world that doesn't always show up for them.

SPIKED BY THE SYSTEM
Comfort is one hell of a sedative.

NICOLA ANNE

INTRO
The Warning Label

Oh hey, fellas.

Before we go any further, here's the truth upfront: this book might make you uncomfortable. Not because you're a bad man, or because I'm here to lecture you, but because we're about to talk honestly about things most men were never invited into - conversations that usually happen after you've left the room. If you're not used to hearing them, they can feel... sharp. Confronting. Maybe even unfair.

But you're here anyway. That says something.

Whatever brought you to these pages - curiosity, frustration, love, confusion, or the subtle pressure of a woman in your life sliding this book across the table - you've taken a step most men don't.

Let me make one thing clear from the start: this isn't a book that's going to pat you on the back just for showing up. It's also not a book that's going to attack you. I'm not interested in making villains out of men. I *am* interested in showing you things that most women see clearly, and most men have never been taught to notice at all.

That gap - that difference in what we each see, fear, assume, excuse, or ignore - is the entire point of this book.
There will be moments when you feel defensive. Moments when you think, "That's not me," or "This is exaggerated," or "Women don't really feel that way." You might catch yourself wanting to argue with me in your head. You might even feel the

instinct to close the book and decide it's not for you.

Stay with it.

Nothing in these pages exists to shame you. I am not interested in guilt, self-pity, or performative chest-beating. What I am interested in is awareness. Because once you see something clearly, you get to choose how you respond. You get to choose the partner, father, friend, colleague, and human you want to be. You get to choose what continues and what stops with *you*.

Here's why this book might sting sometimes: for generations, men have been told a story about how the world works, about how women work, and about what a man's role is supposed to be in all of it. Some of that story helped you. Some of it boxed you in. And some of it quietly trained you to overlook things women have been dealing with every day of their lives.

You didn't create those rules. You inherited them. So did I.

So, when something in these pages feels confronting, remember this: you're not being blamed for history. You're being invited to understand the present.

If you can hold on to that, you'll get something genuinely useful out of this book. Not guilt. Not shame. Clarity. Connection. A way forward that actually works - for you, and for the women you care about.

You'll notice as you read that the examples lean heavily on heterosexual relationships. That's because those are the dynamics I know best, and the ones where these themes appear most consistently. But not every scenario will reflect your experience - and it doesn't need to. These are common patterns, not universal truths. If something doesn't apply to you, don't take it as an accusation; take it as an opportunity to ask why it appears so often for others. And if something does land a little too closely, sit with that.

Whether you're here for your partner, your daughter, your friends, your colleagues, or simply because something inside you is ready to understand things differently, you deserve the whole picture. And the women in your life deserve a man who has it.

This isn't about turning you into someone you're not. It's about showing you what's been happening around you all along and giving you the tools to meet it with awareness rather than frustration or defensiveness.

You've opened the book. You're already ahead of the curve.

At the end of each chapter, I'll prompt you to check in with yourself. What parts made you nod? What parts made you roll your eyes? Whatever you felt is fine. Just notice it. This book isn't about agreeing with everything - it's about paying attention to the stuff that hits a nerve and asking yourself *why*.

Let's keep going. There's a lot to learn - and even more to gain.

CHAPTER ONE
Privilege Unpacked
What it is, what it isn't, and why it matters.

Before we go any further, I want to speak directly to the subject of privilege and where I stand in the middle of all this. I am not interested in pretending I have walked through life battling every obstacle available. I am not interested in polishing myself into some flawless, pure, oppression-free narrator. You deserve honesty, so here it is.

I am a 38-year-old Caucasian woman. I am currently in a heterosexual marriage and have two children. Society reads me as a cis, straight, female, whether or not that is entirely accurate. My family was financially stable when I was growing up. I went to private schools. I am university-educated. I have lived a very privileged life. When I look back at the experiences that have shaped me, the single characteristic that has truly caused any significant oppression has been the fact that I am a woman.

And here is the crucial part. If my limited brushes with oppression have been enough to light a fire under me, enough to push me into writing this book and push back on the systems that restrict women, I can only imagine the inferno burning inside women who face layers of oppression far beyond mine. Women of colour. Women with disabilities. Women who move through a world that rarely treats them with fairness, dignity, or safety.

In that sense, I am not unlike you. Many of their struggles are not ones I share. At times, I find it hard to fully grasp the challenges they face. It would be easy to look the other way. To say, "That is not my fight." To decide that silence is neutral.

But silence is never neutral. When we turn away, we are not stepping out of the issue. We are stepping directly onto the oppressor's side of the line.

My privilege gives me power. And power always comes with responsibility.

Desmond Tutu captured it perfectly: "If you are neutral in situations of injustice, you have chosen the side of the oppressor."

That brings us to you.

Privilege is one of those topics that tends to make people instantly defensive, mostly because privilege often feels invisible to those who have it. People assume that if their life has had any hardship at all, they must not be privileged. But privilege is not the *absence* of struggle. It is the *presence* of advantage.

A huge part of male privilege is the simple reality that it has always been normal for men to take up space in conversations about society, power, work, safety, money and rights. It has always been normal for men to be the majority of leaders. It has always been normal for men to have more voice, more authority, and more cultural leniency. Because it has always been normal, it can be tough to recognise.

Too often, discussions about equality are framed as "women's issues," which results in women sitting in rooms with other women trying to solve problems created by a system in which men are deeply woven. One of the biggest complaints I hear is that men often seem uninterested in participating in the conversation. They feel disconnected from it, or defensive about it, or unsure what to say, so they say nothing at all.

But here is the problem. When men disengage from discussions about equality, the inequality remains. Your silence does not keep you neutral. It keeps you comfortable while women continue to deal with the fallout.

This is privilege in action. The issue isn't intent - it's insulation. You're not evil or malicious. You're just comfortable. And comfort is a powerful sedative.

Many men say, "Why should this involve me? I did not create the problem." Fair question. But not creating something does not mean you do not benefit from it.

Here is the part you might not want to hear. If you are a man, and particularly if you are a straight white man, this conversation may hit you hardest because, for as long as anyone can remember, your demographic has occupied the top of the social ladder. It has been the default. What you say has held weight. What you want has been prioritised.

I know this can feel strange to hear. You might be thinking, "But I am just a regular guy. I work hard. I struggle. I don't feel powerful." And you're probably right. You might never have felt powerful in your own life. You might have been bullied. You might have been poor. You might have had an absent father, a traumatic upbringing, or a difficult adulthood. None of that disappears because of privilege.

Privilege doesn't mean you have had it easy. It simply means *your gender has not made your life harder.*

That distinction matters.

Let's talk about the cost of privilege. Not to make you feel bad, but to help you understand why this conversation is so important. When you have grown up in a system that quietly benefits you, it can feel counterintuitive to want to change it. Supporting a shift that might reduce your advantages feels like being asked to vote yourself out of a job.

IF YOU THINK **TALKING** ABOUT PRIVILEGE IS UNCOMFORTABLE, TRY **LIVING** WITHOUT IT.

But here is the truth. The cost of maintaining the status quo is far higher than the cost of changing it.

Because the alternative is a world where:

Women continue to be paid less.
Women remain afraid to walk alone after dark.
Women face violence at epidemic rates.
Women are judged more on their appearance than their competence.
Women shoulder more unpaid labour, emotional labour, and domestic work.
Women navigate pregnancy, birth, childcare and career sacrifices with less support.
Women continue to be disbelieved, dismissed, or blamed for harm done to them.

Think about how invisible the system can be. In a country like Australia, for example, women still earn around 13-14% less than men on average. It doesn't sound dramatic until you realise that's the difference between breathing room and constant calculation - between being able to save and being one unexpected bill away from panic.

But the system doesn't just hurt women.
It hurts men, too, just in different ways.

It tells men they have to be the provider even when the economy no longer supports single-income households.
It teaches men that anger is acceptable, but sadness is embarrassing.
It pushes men into competition instead of connection.
It convinces men that asking for help makes them weak.
It shames men out of vulnerability, then punishes them for being emotionally distant in their relationships.
It gives men fewer close friendships, fewer support networks, and fewer safe places to talk honestly.
It leaves men with higher suicide rates, higher rates of

untreated depression, and fewer socially acceptable outlets for stress and fear.
It defines masculinity so narrowly that millions of men feel like failures for simply being human.

You've probably felt some of this pressure yourself - maybe without ever linking it back to the system you inherited.

If maintaining privilege means keeping those pressures alive, then privilege is not a perk. It is a problem.

Most men do not want that world. Not for themselves and not for their daughters, wives, mothers or sisters. Which means men have enormous potential to be part of the solution.

When men recognise privilege and choose to challenge it, they shift the system. When they choose to understand rather than defend, or to listen rather than retreat, the world becomes safer and fairer for everyone.

Still not sure what male privilege looks like in practice? Let's look at some examples. These are not accusations. They are simply realities that many men have never consciously noticed.

You are complimented more for your skills and abilities than your appearance.
You grew up seeing countless positive, strong male role models in mainstream media.
Employers do not consider your reproductive capability when hiring you.
When you speak assertively, you are rarely labelled as emotional or abrasive.
You can enter most conversations without being interrupted repeatedly.
Bad moods are attributed to your circumstances, not your hormones.
You can walk alone at night and not actively fear being targeted sexually.

Your clothing choices will never be used against you in cases of assault.
You are not expected to apologise for taking up space.
Your career will probably not be interrupted or judged if you have children.
You can balance work and family without being called selfish.
You are less likely to experience intimate partner violence.
You likely have a higher superannuation balance because you were not expected to take years off for unpaid labour.
You can choose not to have children without being judged as incomplete.
You can enter workplaces without fear of sexual harassment being normalised.
When you get married, no one expects you to change your last name.
Your grooming standards are far less demanding and far less expensive.
If you have multiple sexual partners, no one labels you dirty or undesirable.
Pornography is designed with your pleasure in mind.
When you buy a car or engage a tradesperson, you are less likely to be exploited.
You are unlikely to experience unwanted touching in bars or clubs.
You do not have to manage menstruation while pretending it does not exist.
You are allowed to age without social punishment.

These are not small things. They shape daily life. They shape safety. They shape opportunity.

I am not saying you have experienced all, or any, of these things. And I am not suggesting that they are things only men experience. What I am saying is that men are far more likely to experience these advantages. They represent some ways male privilege operates in the world. I am not suggesting that experiencing these things makes you a bad person, or that men should not have access to good things. I am suggesting that

IF YOU WANT TO SEE THE SYSTEM CLEARLY, LISTEN TO THE PEOPLE IT DOESN'T SERVE.

everyone should have *equal access* to good things.

Male privilege is so deeply woven into our society that most of us are unaware of it until it is pointed out. The first step to meaningful change is noticing it and ensuring that your actions do not come at the expense of others. We get one run at this life. Everyone deserves that run to be safe, dignified and valued.

Here is another way to think about privilege. Imagine society as an old house. None of us designed it, yet we all live in it. Over hundreds of years, certain rooms have been built with strong, even floorboards, while others have been assembled on warped timber that tilts underfoot and is dangerous.

You did not choose your room. You inherited it.

Acknowledging privilege is not blaming you for the architecture. It is recognising that the floor is uneven. Once you see uneven floorboards, pretending the house is level becomes a deliberate choice.

The goal is not to tear the house down. The goal is to repair the foundation so everyone inside it can stand safely without bracing themselves.
You are not being asked to surrender your room. You are being asked to help fix the parts of the house that have been left crooked for too long.

Privilege is not your fault. But choosing to do nothing once you are aware of it *is*.

Awareness does not diminish you. It expands you. It makes your relationships richer. It makes your communication sharper. It makes the women in your life feel seen instead of dismissed. It strengthens trust, connection, intimacy and respect.

That is not a weakness. That is what actual strength looks like.

And it starts with seeing what has always been beneath your feet. Where in your life has the floor felt level to you while someone else was quietly compensating for the slant?

What assumptions have you never had to question? Not because you're unkind - but because the world never required you to.

If you were to look again with a broader lens, what might you see now that you missed before?

CHAPTER TWO
The Man Hater Myth
A closer look at what women's frustration is actually about.

Now that we've dug into how the system tilts the playing field, let's zoom in on what that tilt feels like in real life. Big ideas make sense in theory - but the everyday moments are where most blokes finally see it.

I am a woman with strong views about social justice. I do not hide that. If anything, it walks into the room three steps ahead of me, waving a flag and asking if anyone here has anything they would like to unpack emotionally. Because of that, I have been called many things. Headstrong. Opinionated. Outspoken. Emotional. Aggressive. Rude.

Sometimes people say it lovingly. Sometimes they do not.

Over the years, I have watched the same words land differently when applied to men. When a man is passionate, he is decisive. When he is loud, he is confident. When he is opinionated, he is a leader. When a woman behaves the same, the tone shifts. Suddenly, she is too much. Too hostile. Too angry. Too loud. Too direct. Too confrontational.

One of my close friends went through a brutal divorce a few years ago. It was one of those situations where you could see a woman slowly unravel under the weight of something that was never her fault. Her husband left her after a long trail of affairs. He walked out, but he did so under a very particular assumption. He assumed she would remain the primary caregiver of their children, no questions asked. He assumed he would move out and resume the lifestyle of a bachelor, while she would keep the household running and pick up every piece of the emotional and physical labour that goes into raising small humans.

When she dared question the financial arrangements he proposed, he became emotionally manipulative. He acted as though she were trying to ruin him. As though ensuring the well-being of their children was an attack. As though she were greedy for wanting a fair and equitable division of the assets.

I watched my friend carry the mental load of this chaos while still trying to function in everyday life. The exhaustion. The fear. The financial strain. The emotional whiplash of being abandoned yet still responsible for everything. And I watched him excuse himself from accountability with an ease that was horrifying.

I helped her where I could. I explained what I know of the legal process. I researched options she did not have time to explore. I encouraged her not to rise to provocation. I told her to protect her long-term financial and emotional security. I reminded her she was not unreasonable for wanting fairness.

And for that, he called me a "man-hating bitch".

Not because I hated men. But because he needed a way to dismiss me. To frame me as irrational so he could avoid confronting his own behaviour. To make me the villain so he could protect his comfort. The label became a shortcut. If I could be painted as a man-hater, then every piece of advice I offered became tainted. Every concern became an emotional outburst. Every boundary became extremism.

Ah yes. The man-hating feminist. Possibly the most convenient stereotype ever invented. It is a cultural cheat code. A fast track to invalidating everything a woman says. A way to avoid the discomfort of accountability without ever having to engage in the substance of her argument.

Label her as a man-hater, and suddenly, she is too irrational to listen to. Too extreme to be taken seriously. Too emotional to trust. Too damaged to be credible. Her anger becomes the problem instead of the situation that caused it.

This stereotype silences women long before their words can do any actual damage to the status quo.

My experience of this wasn't an outlier. Plenty of women shared almost identical versions of this story when I asked them about backlash for calling out bad behaviour. The details change, but the reaction - dismiss, minimise, reframe her as the problem - shows up everywhere.

It is remarkable how often men who genuinely believe in equality still fall into this trap. They agree that women should be safe. They agree women deserve equal rights. They agree that violence is unacceptable. And yet, the moment a woman expresses anger, frustration, exhaustion or fear, these same men recoil. They want her to be "reasonable". Quiet. Polite. Controlled. Calm.

They want women to talk about injustice without expressing any emotion about it. They want women to discuss fear without sounding afraid. They want women to lay out their trauma in a tone that will not make men uncomfortable.

It is an impossible demand.

This is not a new tactic. Women who fought for the right to vote were called hysterical. Women who demanded access to education were called unfeminine. Women who sought equality in the workforce were labelled radicals. The pattern is identical: discredit the woman so you do not have to confront the system she is challenging.

It's easier to attack the tone than face the truth.

Let me be clear about something. Most women do not hate men. In fact, many women love men deeply. Women have fathers, brothers, sons, partners, friends and colleagues they care for. The idea that women en masse despise men is absurd. If women genuinely hated men, the tension would be visible everywhere.

What women hate are certain behaviours. Systems. Patterns. Women hate the way their safety depends on men's behaviour more than their own. They hate the mental load. The emotional labour. The double standards. The dismissal. The objectification. The way male violence shapes every part of their lives.

Women do not hate men.

Women hate the conditions created *by* men.

But here is where the emotional divide becomes clear. When women criticise behaviour, men often hear criticism of themselves personally. They hear women say "men" and think "me." They hear anger and assume hostility. They hear frustration and assume blame.

Women are not blaming individual men. They are naming collective patterns.

Women are not saying, "You did this." They are saying, "This keeps happening everywhere, and it affects us constantly."

Men hear accusation.
Women are describing reality.

The difference in interpretation is enormous.

There is also a stark difference in stakes.

When women criticise men, men feel wounded. Offended. Embarrassed. Defensive. Their pride takes a hit.

But when men hate women, women get harmed.

When men hate women, women get stalked, assaulted, controlled or killed.

Women know this. They live with that knowledge every day. So, when they express fear or caution, they are not insulting all men. They are acknowledging the statistical reality.

Here is the uncomfortable truth:
Most men are safe, but women have no reliable way of knowing which ones.

This is why women are cautious. This is why they scan rooms. This is why they do not walk alone in certain places. This is why they hesitate before trusting men they do not know.

Not because they believe all men are dangerous.
But because they cannot identify the dangerous ones until it is too late.

The phrase "not all men" comes up frequently when women talk about their experiences. It is usually offered as reassurance, but it functions more like interruption. Women already know it is not all men. What women also know is that *all* women have been affected.

You would be hard pressed to find a woman who has not been harassed, objectified, dismissed, belittled, frightened or threatened by a man at some point. The phrase "Not all men" does nothing to protect women. It does everything to protect male *feelings*.

It shifts the conversation away from women's safety and turns it into a discussion about men's reputations. It reframes women's trauma as an insult rather than a warning. It prioritises men's comfort over women's lived experience.

We will come back to this later, but in general, if you want to support women, there is a very simple rule:
Stop defending men and start listening to women.

Now, let us address the idea that feminism is anti-male. It is not. Feminism is anti-harm. Anti-inequality. Anti-violence. Feminism is not here to eradicate men. Feminism is here to eliminate the conditions that damage both women *and* men.

Patriarchy restricts men, too. It dictates that men must be providers, leaders, protectors and stoic pillars of strength. It teaches men to suppress vulnerability, which eventually isolates them emotionally. It teaches men that dominance equals worth, and softness equals weakness.

Patriarchy harms men by cutting off half their emotional range. In fact, one in six Australian men don't have a single close friend they could open up to - proof this conversation isn't just for women's benefit. Men die by suicide at four times the rate of women. If talking about gender feels uncomfortable, the cost of *not* talking about it is a hell of a lot worse.

Feminism is not trying to strip men of anything. It is trying to give men back the emotional, relational and human freedoms they were taught to avoid.

When women fight the system, they are not fighting men. They are fighting an inheritance they didn't ask for.

This is why the stereotype of the man-hating feminist collapses under scrutiny. Women who challenge inequality are not trying to punish men. They are trying to survive men who have never faced consequences. They are trying to protect themselves. They are trying to build a world where men can be partners instead of threats.

If anything, men benefit tremendously when feminism succeeds. They get to be emotionally honest. They get to share domestic and parenting responsibilities without stigma. They get to be full humans, not representatives of a rigid stereotype.

That is not oppression. That is liberation.

Returning to the story of my friend's divorce, the moment her ex called me a man-hater became a perfect example of how the stereotype functions. He needed a villain because acknowledging his behaviour would have required self-reflection. It was easier to attack my character than to confront his actions. Easier to call me extreme than admit he had been unfair. Easier to blame me than take responsibility.

This is the heart of the man-hater accusation. It is almost always used when a man feels confronted by a truth he would rather avoid. It allows him to avoid discomfort. To avoid accountability. To avoid himself.

Calling a woman a man-hater is not a factual observation. It is a defence mechanism.

And here is the important part. Secure men do not fear women's anger. Emotionally mature men do not fall apart at the suggestion that they could grow. Men who understand power do not interpret criticism as hatred.

Most women are not asking men to apologise for existing. They are asking men to listen. To understand. To reflect. To stop making women the enemy whenever women articulate the conditions they live under.

When a woman raises her voice, she is not expressing hatred of men. She is expressing a fear of harm.

When a woman sets boundaries, she is not rejecting men. She is protecting herself.

When a woman calls out disrespect, she is not attacking

manhood. She is defending dignity.

These are not acts of hatred. These are acts of survival.

Let me speak directly to you, the man reading this.

If you feel uncomfortable when women talk about male violence, that discomfort is not proof that women hate men. It is proof that you are encountering experiences you have never had to consider before, or that you recognise some of those behaviours in yourself or your male friends, and that recognition is confronting.

If you feel defensive when women express anger, remind yourself that anger is often the last stage of a long history of patience. Women do not get angry out of nowhere. They get angry after years of politeness failed them.

If you feel blamed when women talk about harmful male behaviour, remember that women are speaking about patterns, not individuals. They are trying to prevent future harm, not punish men who have done nothing wrong.

Your job is not to defend men as a collective. Your job is to listen to women as individuals.

Stay present. Stay curious. Stay open. Ask questions instead of shutting down. Hear what women are *saying* rather than what you fear they might be *implying*.

The truth is simple: when women speak up, they are not trying to tear men down. They are trying to build a world that keeps them alive.

That is not hatred. That is hope.

Think of a moment when a woman's anger struck you as "too much." What story did you tell yourself about her in that moment? And what story might she have been carrying beneath the surface?

If you sat with both truths at the same time - yours and hers - what would shift? What becomes possible when you stop defending against the emotion and start listening for what shaped it?

A lot of men hear conversations about women's safety or frustration and assume they're being positioned as the enemy. But that defensiveness is often rooted in something deeper: the fear that the old foundations are shifting. Women are increasingly financially independent, socially supported, and able to walk away from relationships that don't feel equal. And when the dynamic changes, the story men were raised on starts to feel uncertain. That's where we're going next.

CHAPTER THREE
From Need to Want
Understanding the past so the present makes more sense.

I have been married to my husband for over 15 years. We have had moments that could be bottled and sold as proof that humans are capable of great love. We have also had moments where we could barely look at each other. Every long relationship has both, but not every relationship comes with genuine turning points.

There was a brief period when we separated. It was not dramatic. No screaming matches. No broken plates. No public declarations. It was quieter than that. It was the kind of separation that arrives slowly, in the small gaps between conversations, in the heavy silence at the end of the day, in the feeling that we were no longer reaching for each other but living side by side like two people who had accidentally boarded the wrong train.

During that time, I had to figure out what I actually wanted. Not what I was supposed to want. Not what marriage books tell women they should want. Not what society says a good mother or good wife should want. I had to figure out whether I wanted a relationship at all.

At first, I worried I would return to the relationship for the wrong reasons. For the safety. For the comfort. For the routine. For the shared bills. For the predictable rhythm of a life already built. But the more honest I became with myself, the more I realised I did not actually need those things from him. I could already provide them for myself.

I was educated. I could generate my own income. I could pay for my own housing. I had friends and family who provided emotional support. I could build a life that was safe and secure without relying on a man to anchor it.

Once that clicked, the fear dissolved.

What I missed was not the safety net. What I missed was the companionship. The friendship. The shared humour. The feeling of having someone who wanted to walk through life with me, not someone who happened to be walking beside me. I missed having a partner to celebrate with and a partner to sit with when everything felt heavy.

It dawned on me that my husband was not the person I needed. He was the person I wanted.

That distinction changed everything. It created a foundation that felt stronger than anything built on obligation or dependency. It allowed us to rebuild our relationship not as two people clinging to each other for survival, but as two people choosing each other deliberately, fully aware that either of us could walk away and still land on our feet.

It was not an isolated or final decision. There have been many more ebbs and flows in our relationship since, and there will be many more to come – and it may be that one day we decide we no longer want this relationship in the form that is currently packaged. And that's okay.

This experience introduced a realisation that has rippled across almost every conversation I have had with women since.

Women didn't suddenly wake up one day and decide men were optional. This shift didn't come from TikTok or "girl dinners." It came from a long, messy history where women literally had no choice but to rely on men for money, safety, housing, reputation - even survival. This chapter isn't about your current relationship. It's about the system women had to push against for generations before they ever got to a point where they could stand on their own feet. To understand where things are now, you've got to understand what women had to break out of first.

When I asked women what they wished men understood, one theme came through more loudly than anything else. It was not sex. It was not romance. It was not domestic labour. It was not emotional intelligence.

It was this:
"We do not need you. We want you."

This seems simple, but it is a seismic shift in gender dynamics. For most of history, women needed men to survive. The world was designed that way. Property laws. Voting rights. Financial restrictions. Work opportunities. Social structures. Marriage expectations. Everything pointed toward dependence. A woman alone was not simply single. She was worthless. She was vulnerable. And the world made sure she knew it.

It wasn't until 1983 that marital rape became illegal in Australia. In the 1970s, women still needed a man's signature to get a loan. Women did not gain no-fault divorce rights until 1975.

This is recent history. Men held all the resources. Men made the rules. Men owned the property. Men controlled the finances. Men had access to education and opportunity. Women gained both by attaching themselves to a man.

Needing a man was not romantic. It was practical.

Before we go further, it's important to acknowledge something men often feel but rarely say out loud: the pressure to provide is real. Men haven't exactly been skipping through fields without expectations of their own. You've been raised to believe your worth is tied to earning, performing, achieving, and being the stable one.

And when women become more financially independent, it can feel like the ground shifts underneath you.

So, when men say women are becoming too independent, what they really mean is that the system is no longer protecting their default position as the provider or the selector. Women have options now. Women have financial autonomy. Women can raise children alone. Women can thrive alone. Women can design entire lives that men do not automatically fit into.

That shift is confronting for a lot of men. Of course it is. If you have grown up being told that your value lies in being a provider, a protector or a head of the household, then hearing that women no longer need those things from you can feel like someone poked a hole directly into your identity.

Many men hear, "I do not *need* you", and assume it means "I do not *value* you."

But the opposite is true. If a woman chooses a man despite not needing him, that is the highest accolade a man can receive. It means she wants him for who he is, not what he provides.

Men often see independence as rejection. Women experience independence as dignity.

Among the most frustrating realities for women is the way their independence gets reframed as hostility. When women talk about not needing a man, many men react as though they have been insulted.

"She must hate men."
"She is too difficult."
"She is bitter."
"She is wounded."
"She is trying to prove something."

No, she is simply free.

Women do not start their day thinking, "How can I undermine the male ego today?" They start it by managing jobs, housework, parenting, schedules, friendships, and emotional labour. If a woman articulates that she can do all this without a man, that is not emasculation. That is the truth.

Independence is not a threat. It is a baseline.

Men who depend on women needing them instead of wanting them often find modern relationships hard. Not because women have become unreasonable, but because the rules changed and many men were never taught to adapt.

If your sense of worth was built on being needed, then being wanted will feel unfamiliar at first. It requires a unique skill set. Not dominance but partnership. Not authority but communication. Not entitlement but reciprocity.

And here is the part men rarely consider. Women becoming independent has been the most significant act of love men could ever receive. Women are no longer forced to stay in relationships out of fear, finances or social expectation. If a woman chooses you, it is because she genuinely wants you in her life.

That is not a threat to masculinity. It is a validation of it.

Many men feel a sense of panic when they hear women say they want equal partnership rather than traditional roles.

This panic reveals something interesting. It shows how deeply the system has sold men short about their own humanity. Men have been told for generations that their worth lies in their utility.

Be strong.
Be tough.
Earn more.

Protect her.
Provide stability.
Solve the problem.
Never break.
Never fail.
Never feel.
Never rely on anyone.

This is a suffocating box disguised as a pedestal.

When women say they do not need men to provide these things anymore, some men feel robbed. But this is actually an invitation. It invites men to explore areas of themselves they were never allowed to value.

Men can offer so much more than money, strength or security. Men can provide humour, companionship, intellect, vulnerability, creativity, gentleness, insight, curiosity, affection and emotional availability.

Women want partners, not supervisors. They want connection, not control. They want collaboration, not caretaking.

Men do not lose value when women become independent. Men finally have the chance to be valued for who they are, not just for what they earn.

Many women have spent years learning to be self-sufficient. It was a survival skill at first, but it became a source of pride. So, when women say they are independent, it is rarely a criticism of men. It is a celebration of themselves.

It is a rejection of the idea that their worth is tied to a partner. It is a statement that they refuse to enter relationships out of fear or pressure. It is an affirmation that love, when it comes, should be chosen willingly, not needed desperately.

Women are not proud of being alone. They are proud of being

capable.

A lot of men misunderstand this.

They think independence means women do not want connection. That is not true. Women want connection deeply. But they want a connection with someone who is genuinely there, not someone who sees her as a project or a possession. Independence makes women better partners because it removes the weight of obligation. It makes relationships lighter, freer, and more honest. No one is trapped. Everyone is choosing each other intentionally.

This is what modern partnership looks like.

There is also a historical shadow attached to this conversation. For generations, the worst insult society could throw at a woman was that she would end up "old and alone." The assumption was that a woman's value depended entirely on being chosen by a man.

That shadow still lingers. It shows up in jokes about spinsters and cat ladies. In pitying comments about single women. In the way people speak about divorced women as though they failed at something essential.

But women have stopped buying that narrative. They have seen too many examples of women trapped in relationships that drained them, harmed them or erased them. Being alone is not the worst fate. Being in a relationship that makes you feel alone, threatened, or vulnerable is.

Women do not fear being alone. They fear being unrecognised, undervalued or unsafe.

Men, on the other hand, often fear being unnecessary. That fear is understandable. But it is not the burden of women to soothe it. It is the responsibility of men to redefine what makes them valuable.

Your worth is not measured by how much a woman depends on you. It is measured by how you show up when she does not need you at all.

Men and women can walk together, support each other, love deeply and build extraordinary lives. But they can only do that when both people are free.

Choice is the foundation of healthy love. Needing someone is not the same as loving them.

When she says she does not need a man, she is not rejecting men. She is rejecting the idea that she must rely on one to be whole.

That is the difference between dependence and partnership. Between control and collaboration. Between obligation and love.

A woman who does not need you is not a threat to your masculinity. She is proof that if she chooses you, it is real.

There is no greater compliment.

What kind of bloke do you want to be when you're standing next to someone who's there by choice, not dependence?

CHAPTER FOUR

More Than a List

A guide to what's happening behind the scenes in your own home.

A little while ago, I was pacing around the living room, running through the week in my head, trying to connect twelve different scheduling threads, four household tasks, three upcoming appointments, two kid-related deadlines, a work project, and the vague awareness that something important was happening on Friday that I had not written down but absolutely needed to remember.

My husband looked at me, saw the mild chaos radiating from my face, and said the sentence a supportive man often says:

"I can help. Just write me a list - I'm more than happy to do it."

He meant it.
He genuinely meant it.
He was offering help.
He was being a good partner.
He was responding exactly as men are taught to respond:
Tell me what you need, and I'll do it.

The problem was not his willingness.
The problem was that writing the list was 80% of the work.

He did not realise that by the time I had written the list, I had already done the organising, prioritising, remembering, predicting, coordinating, budgeting, planning, sequencing and anticipating. The list was simply the visible part. The doing was mechanical. The thinking was the labour.

He was offering to carry the luggage.

But I had already mapped the entire journey, chosen the route, bought the tickets, checked the weather, booked the accommodation, and made sure the kids had snacks.

His offer was well-intentioned – but it arrived at the end of the process rather than the beginning.

Women are socialised to live at the beginning of things - to anticipate, plan, prevent, and track. Men, meanwhile, are often socialised to wait until the end, stepping in only when a task becomes visible or concrete.

This is the mental load.

The mental work is not about who does more.
It is about who notices first.

Men tend to engage when asked.
Women tend to engage before asking is necessary.

Women see the spill on the counter.
Men notice it once it reaches natural disaster levels.

Women know when the dishwasher is almost full.
Men know when the dishwasher physically cannot contain another molecule of crockery.

Women remember the dentist appointment three weeks out.
Men remember it when someone hands them the keys and says, "We need to leave now."

Women buy gifts for birthdays, weddings, anniversaries, family events, Secret Santa gifts, school raffles, sports coaches, and the neighbour's child's birthday party.
Men show up gratefully holding whatever she purchased.

Women track the household inventory: the toilet paper, the

milk, the bin bags, the laundry powder, the snacks, the toothpaste, the band-aids, the pet food, the medications, the hand wash, the vegetables, the light bulbs.

Men open the fridge and say, "We're out of milk," as though they've just discovered a rare geological phenomenon.

Women pre-empt emotional needs, social dynamics, upset children, interpersonal tensions, upcoming stress periods, and minor domestic frictions.
Men respond once those things are already happening.

The mental load is invisible until no one is managing it.
Then suddenly the absence becomes obvious.

The mental load is not about what women *do*.
It is about what women *carry*. And cognitive labour studies show women carry around 70% of the "thinking" work at home - the stuff no one sees.

Let me be clear: this is not about competence.
Men are capable.
Men are intelligent.
Men are skilled.
Men can run countries, companies, teams, entire industries.

But domestic labour runs on a different operating system.
One that men were not socialised to download.

Girls are taught from childhood to anticipate.
To multitask.
To monitor.
To remember.
To check on.
To prepare.
To smooth over.
To plan ahead.

THE BAR IS NOT PERFECTION. THE BAR IS **PARTICIPATION**.

Boys are taught to focus on the task at hand.
Direct.
Linear.
Singular.
Straightforward.

Women are praised for being *thoughtful.*
Men are praised for being *helpful*.

Women *carry* the load.
Men *respond* to the load.

Both think they are 50% of the equation.
But one is forecasting, organising and coordinating the entire equation before it even reaches the "doing" stage.

The cognitive load is like running the world's quietest project management firm out of your own brain.

There are no holidays.
There is no sick leave.
No one applauds your scheduling skills.
No one sees the internal spreadsheet.
It is a full-time job you are not recognised or paid for, and you cannot outsource because you are the only one who knows all the moving pieces.

It is remembering the school hat.
It is knowing where the scissors are.
It's ordering the book lists.
It is knowing which child hates which food this week.
It is knowing the pet's vaccination date.
It is knowing the phone plan expires in November.
It is knowing the towels need replacing.
It is knowing the teacher likes almond chocolate.
It is knowing the last of the wrapping paper was used at Christmas.
It is knowing the washing machine has been making that weird

noise again.

And here is the kicker:
If a woman drops the ball, the world notices.
If a man drops the ball, the world asks, "But, did she remind him?"

Women are expected to remember everything.
Men are expected to 'help' when prompted.

No wonder so many women eventually feel like managers, not partners.

But not because men are lazy. Men do not see the invisible labour because the system has *trained them not to*. And women are exhausted from pretending the labour is light.

Emotional labour is the close cousin of the mental load.
It is the work of smoothing the rough edges of life for everyone else.

It is the job of caring, gauging, supporting, noticing, adjusting, softening and anticipating the needs of others.

Men often assume emotional labour is just listening.
Women know it is the constant, tiny, uncredited art of maintaining relational stability.

It is remembering who had a bad week.
It is knowing when someone needs space.
It is organising birthday cards, group gifts, dinner plans, and thank-you messages.
It is checking in with relatives.
It is carrying the household atmosphere.
It is mediating conflict.
It is predicting moods.
It is making sure the kids feel secure.
It is reminding your partner to call his mum.

It is knowing when to step lightly.
It is knowing when to step in.

Men do emotional labour, too.
Just in different ways.
Often loudly.
Often visibly.
Often in bursts.

Women tend to do it quietly, constantly, frequently, and without language for the workload.

This is why women often seem "more stressed."
They are not more stressed.
They are carrying more.

Not more tasks.
More responsibility for remembering the tasks.
The labour is not the chore.
It is the ongoing awareness that the chore needs to be done.

Many men think the solution is simple:
Just tell me what you need.
Give me a list.
Ask me to help.
I'm more than happy to do it.

Men say this with love.
With sincerity.
With pride.
They see it as partnership.

But to women, this solution sounds like:
"I am happy to execute tasks, but you remain the manager."

Asking for help takes work.
Noticing what needs doing takes work.
Tracking the moving parts takes work.

Delegating takes work.
And if she has to tell him every time, she is not sharing the load.
She is supervising it.

The difference between helping and partnering is initiative.

Helping is doing what she asks.
Partnering is noticing without being asked.

Helping is completing the list.
Partnering is co-creating the list.

Helping says, "Tell me what to do."
Partnering is asking yourself, "What needs to be done?"

Helping is labour.
Partnering is leadership.

Women do not want assistants.
They want allies.

The goal of this chapter is not to guilt-trip men.
It is to give men eyesight. None of this behaviour is hardwired.
It's conditioning - passed down quietly, absorbed automatically, and rarely questioned.

Most men are not avoiding the mental load.
They are simply unaware of it.
It is invisible until someone hands them the metaphorical glasses.

Here's what women mean when they talk about the mental load. It's not the task itself—it's the constant upstream thinking that happens before the task even begins.

Take something simple: organising a birthday present for one of the kids' friends.
The visible *task*? Buying the present

The invisible part? Everything that happens silently in the background:

Knowing the birthday is coming
Knowing the child's age
Knowing the child's interests
Knowing the party date
Knowing the wrapping situation
Knowing the card situation
Knowing whether the parents prefer educational or loud toys

By the time you say, "Just tell me what to do," we've already done fifteen invisible steps you didn't even know were there. And again, this isn't about blame. This is the architecture of the house we've all grown up in. The uneven floorboard here is that women have been trained to anticipate, prevent, soothe, plan, and remember, while men have been trained to wait for instruction.

When she says, "I'm overwhelmed," the mental load includes:
Sixteen things she hasn't mentioned.
Ten things she is holding together.
Four upcoming commitments.
And the pressure of having to pretend it is all manageable.

Let's go back to the analogy of the uneven house. Women spend their days checking the floorboards without even realising they're doing it - testing for weak spots, catching potential collapses before they happen. By the time a man is ready to secure a new plank, she has already identified the one causing the problem, measured the size, ordered the materials and organised to be home for the delivery.

If men want to truly share the mental load, it begins by noticing more.
Noticing the shared spaces.
Noticing the household rhythms.
Noticing the undone tasks.

Noticing the invisible shifts.
Noticing before she has to ask.

Noticing is not mind-reading.
It is partnership.

Men sometimes fear that taking on the mental load will require them to become hyper-organised domestic machines.

It will not.
It requires becoming present.
Nothing more.

Instead of assuming she has it handled, men can assume she is overloaded.
Because she is.
Most women are.
Even the ones who look effortless.

Sharing the mental load means stepping into the role of co-pilot rather than well-meaning passenger.

It means taking initiative without waiting for a detailed request.
It means remembering without being constantly reminded.
It means caring about the invisible stuff, not because you love chores, but because you love the person who has been carrying them by default.

She did not ask to take on the entire household administration.
She is not 'naturally' or biologically more suited to it. As a man, you are not incapable of initiative, prioritisation and organisation—in fact, I would hazard a guess that you demonstrate all those skills regularly in your workplace or sports team.

Similarly, emotional labour is not a *feminine* skill.
It is a *human* skill that women carry because men were trained not to.

When men step into this labour willingly, relationships transform.
Not because women finally relax.
But because the relationship finally becomes balanced.

Women stop managing the entire ecosystem.
Men stop waiting for instructions.
Everything flows more easily.
There is less resentment.
Less pressure.
Less exhaustion.
More connection.
More respect.
More partnership.

The thinking work is the architecture of daily life.
Sharing it is the architecture of a healthy relationship.

The mental load is not about tasks.
It is about responsibility.

The emotional labour is not about intensity.
It is about awareness.

Men do not need to become domestic clairvoyants.
They simply need to participate in the invisible work, rather than wait for it to *become visible*.

Take some time to think about your average day. How many things "just happen" because someone else remembered them? Now imagine you took ownership of even one of those things before anyone asked. What would that look like? And how would it change the load on the person who usually keeps it all in their head?

NOTHING PROTECTS INEQUALITY MORE EFFECTIVELY THAN MEN WHO THINK THEY'RE NEUTRAL.

CHAPTER FIVE
Incompetent Weaponry
Understanding the gap between ability and willingness.

I was having coffee with a friend recently when she told me a story so perfectly on-brand for long-term relationships.

She said she'd asked her husband to change the baby. A straightforward everyday task. One that didn't require breasts or a vagina.

A few minutes later, he walked back in, handed her the baby with the proud posture of a man who believed he had completed a major contribution to the household, and said, "All done."

Except the nappy... wasn't done.
At all.

The thing was hanging on by a single side tab. It was so loose it looked like the baby had borrowed someone else's pants two sizes too big. There was a visible gap. A gap big enough to guarantee that if the baby so much as sneezed, they'd be deep in a situation that would require gloves and a sizeable volume of bleach.

She blinked at it.
Then blinked at him.
Then blinked again at the nappy, which was sliding south by the second.

Trying to be calm, she said, "Babe... this is falling off him."

He looked genuinely affronted.

"I tried," he said. "You're such a perfectionist. This is why I don't even bother doing it half the time. You're never happy."

She stared at him, baby on her hip, nappy threatened to abandon ship.
She said, "It's not perfectionism. It's gravity. Gravity is going to take this entire nappy to the floor."

He shrugged defensively.
"Well, sorry I'm not as good as you. I give up. Nothing I do is ever right."

She told me she stood there holding a baby who now needed a second nappy change, listening to her husband act like he was the victim of unrealistic expectations, when the only expectation she had was that the nappy remain attached to the baby.

We both laughed at this absolutely absurd turn of events, but she wasn't really laughing.

She was tired.
Not tired of nappies.
Tired of the pattern.

Because sometimes the problem isn't that he did it wrong.
It's that doing it wrong becomes a strategy for not having to do it at all. Ever.

If Chapter 4 was about the *thinking*, this one's about the *doing* - or, more accurately, the "not really doing it properly so someone else steps in" part.

Weaponised incompetence is one of those phrases that often makes men bristle, which is understandable. Nobody wants to believe they are using incompetence as a tactic. Most men aren't. Most men genuinely think they're trying. Most men believe a loose nappy is simply a loose nappy, not a symptom of something bigger.

But in relationships, patterns matter.

Weaponised incompetence is not about being bad at things. It is about acting less capable than you are, so the responsibility shifts, silently and permanently, to someone else. Sometimes it's accidental. Sometimes it's behavioural muscle memory. Sometimes it's the path of least resistance. Rarely is it malicious. But it is almost always damaging.

It's important to understand that these moments aren't about intelligence. They're about practice and expectation. When someone hasn't been required to build a skill, they internalise the idea that they can't do it, or that someone else will do it better. That belief becomes self-fulfilling.

Women know this pattern instantly because they see the progression.

One task done poorly.
Then another.
Then a phase of "I can't do it how you like it." Or, "Your expectations are just too high."
Then the compliments that double as opt-outs: "You're so much better at this than I am."
Then, eventually, the responsibility quietly lands on her plate.

All while he walks away believing he doesn't have the same skill set.

It isn't that he's incapable.
It's that incompetence *pays off*.

I want to make it clear that this isn't *every* man, but it's a common enough pattern that most women will recognise it instantly.

The real trouble with weaponised incompetence is that it shifts the load without anyone ever having a conversation about it. It takes something that was supposed to be shared between two adults and slowly redistributes it until one person becomes the household's unofficial project manager.

Men often think they're helping.
Women know they're supervising.

He completes a task.
She completes the corrections.

He says, "I tried."
She says, "I know," while quietly fixing the entire thing.

He believes he is contributing.
She is doing double the work.

She didn't sign up for this arrangement.
It just... happened.
One poorly executed task at a time.

Over months or years, the consequences add up. It is not a single loose nappy that pushes a woman to breaking point. It is the fiftieth one. It is the sense that she can never entirely rely on him to take something and run with it. It is the cumulative erosion of trust in his follow-through.

And nothing destroys desire quite like feeling you are raising two people instead of one.

This behaviour doesn't show up just in nappies. It surfaces everywhere:
The dishwasher loaded like a Tetris board designed by a rogue raccoon.
The laundry "folded" in a way that somehow added wrinkles.
The grocery shopping done so incompletely that she still has to go out again.

MOST MEN AREN'T MALICIOUS. THEY'RE **COMFORTABLE** AND COMFORT MAKES WILLFUL IGNORANCE EASY.

The kids' bags packed with exactly none of the things they need.
The bin taken out, but the bin liner left off, like the job ended early because of unforeseen fatigue.

To him, these moments seem minor.
To her, they mean she cannot trust that handing something over means it is actually handled.

Men often interpret this frustration as criticism.
Women interpret it as reality.

She's not expecting perfection.
She's expecting competence.

Most men aren't consciously weaponising anything. They simply grew up in systems that let them lean on incompetence because someone else always filled the gap.

Boys are rarely taught the mechanics of domestic life.
Boys are not encouraged to practice these tasks.
Boys are not rewarded for learning them.
Boys are not expected to carry the invisible parts of a household.

Then boys become men, and the smallest domestic task becomes a performance rather than a standard, expected part of adulthood.

He tries to help.
He fumbles.
She steps in.
He looks relieved.
She looks tired.
He thinks, "Well, she's just better at it."
She thinks, "I don't have the option of *not* being 'better at it.'"

This is how the dynamic sets like concrete.

This chapter is not about suggesting men are in any way incompetent. It is suggesting that men tend to have grown up in a house where someone else was constantly patching the flooring before they felt the wobble. If you never feel the tilt, you never learn to balance.

The fix is not about demanding perfection.
Nor is it about shaming men.
Shame doesn't create competence.
Practice does.

And competence is not built through exposure.
It is built through engagement.

Men learn new skills all the time in every other area of life.

The same focus you bring to rebuilding a carburettor, sorting out your fantasy footy picks, or troubleshooting your mate's dodgy Wi-Fi is more than enough to learn how the household runs.

When researchers compared "too hard at home" tasks with similar ones at work, men performed just fine. The issue is not, and was never, ability.

It is easier to rely on her.
It is less mentally taxing to defer.
It is safer to be the "helper" than the person accountable for outcomes.

But ease is not *partnership*.

Weaponised incompetence is so poisonous because it builds resentment.
Not instantly.
Not dramatically.
But slowly.

Women do not resent men for doing things badly.
They resent men for never getting better at them.

A mistake once is human.
A mistake repeated fifty times is a strategy.

Especially when the mistake always results in the other person taking over.

When a man repeatedly hands back tasks in a mess, he is not signalling a lack of skill.
He is signalling a lack of responsibility.

And if there is one thing women need in long-term relationships, it is a partner they can count on.
Not sometimes.
Not occasionally.
Not when it's convenient.
Consistently.

Dependability is not a personality trait.
It is a practice.

So, what does responsibility actually look like in action?

It looks like _doing what you say you'll do, when you say you'll do it._

It looks like trying again instead of giving up.
It looks like fixing your mistake rather than standing back dramatically and declaring yourself a tragic failure.
It looks like learning the household systems instead of asking the same questions every day.
It looks like improving, even slightly, instead of fossilising your incompetence.
It looks like listening to feedback without turning it into a personal attack.
It looks like doing the task from start to finish, not halfway and

then surrendering.
It looks like approaching household duties with the same curiosity and effort men apply to hobbies, sports, careers and interests.

Responsibility is not complicated.
It is simply the willingness to stay.

It means not handing a woman a half-done job six months after it was due and calling it a contribution.

Men who take responsibility become deeply attractive because nothing is sexier than a man who can be trusted to do what he said he would do.
A man who follows through.
A man who tries again.
A man who learns.
A man who builds competence with time.
A man who does not wilt at the first sign of domestic challenge.

This is not weakness.
This is maturity.

The truth is simple: women do not want to carry all the competence in a relationship.
They do not want to be the household CEO.
They do not want to train, supervise, remind, correct and redo endlessly.

They want a partner who sees the work.
A partner who steps up.
A partner who does not weaponise incompetence to escape responsibility.
A partner who grows instead of retreats.

When men step into complete competence, the relationship feels less like work and more like teamwork.
There is less resentment.

Less conflict.
Less emotional distance.
More ease.
More respect.
More closeness.

Competence is connection.

It signals to a woman:
"You can trust me."
"You can rely on me."
"I won't hand things back to you."
"I am your equal, not your dependent."

Be honest with yourself: is there a job you've pretended to be bad at, avoided, or "forgotten" enough times that someone else stepped in? No judgement - just notice it. Then ask: What would happen if I actually tried with this one? How would the vibe at home shift if I stopped dodging it?

Weaponised incompetence ends where responsibility begins.
One choice at a time.
One task at a time.
One nappy tab, correctly fastened, at a time.

CHAPTER SIX
Beauty IS the Beast
A look at the emotional toll of being constantly assessed.

As a mother to both a son and a daughter, I have had a front-row seat to the subtle differences in how people treat boys and girls. I am not talking about the overblown stereotypes that people loudly claim they no longer believe in. I am talking about the small, invisible moments that accumulate quietly until one day you realise your children have been ushered into two very different versions of the world.

My son is now six. My daughter is four. They are both still little, both still curious, both delightful in ways only small children can be. And yet, already, the world is interacting with them differently.

Any parent will be familiar with the anxiety surrounding milestones. Rolling by four months. Sitting by six. Walking by twelve. Five words by eighteen. We get these lists handed to us by nurses, doctors, online forums and competitive parents who swear their baby recited Shakespeare before solids. It is an exhausting checklist that somehow dictates your self-worth for a while, until you realise children do not care at all about timelines.

With my son, every milestone was met with celebration from the world around him. "He is so clever." "He is such a smart boy." "He is so advanced." Even strangers in the shops would call him cheeky, observant, or bright. People commented on what he could do.

Two years later, my daughter arrived. If I had a dollar for every time someone called her "beautiful," "pretty," "gorgeous," "stunning," or "a little doll," I would be typing this from a private yacht with my feet up. Her eyes, her hair, her curls, her cheeks. People adore her appearance. People comment on what she looks like, not who she is or what she is capable of.

The compliments are not malicious. They are innocent, reflexive, automatic. That is precisely the issue. Without thinking, we praise girls for beauty and boys for capability. Without realising it, we begin shaping a girl's identity around her appearance years before she even knows what appearance means.

I catch myself doing it too. I am a woman who speaks loudly and passionately about the impact of beauty standards. I know the pressure. I know how toxic it can be. Yet I still find myself admiring my daughter's curls before I admire her strength. I point out her big blue eyes before I point out her independence.

My daughter is fierce. She is brave. She is determined. She is the child who will climb higher than she should and glare at me if I try to help. She is fiery in all the ways that will serve her well as a woman. These are the qualities that will shape her life. But the world around her sees the curls first.

It terrifies me.

Because I know where that path leads.

The beauty industry is among the most complex traps women navigate, often without realising they are even in it. Women grow up drowning in imagery designed to make them feel inadequate. It is everywhere. Billboards. Movies. Ads. Influencers. TikTok. Gym culture. Porn culture. Fitness culture. Skincare culture. There is no escaping it.

It is not just traditional advertising anymore. It is woven into the rhythm of everyday life. You open your phone to check a message, and there, sandwiched between your friend's birthday selfie and your cousin's baby photos, is a perfectly edited woman selling you the belief that you should look more like her.

The standard is impossible. Bigger breasts. Smaller waists. Fuller lips. Blemish free skin. Shiny hair. Sculpted jawlines. Thicker lashes. Smaller pores. Longer legs. Flat stomachs. Endless youth.

The most horrifying part is that many women genuinely believe this pursuit is empowering. They say they got the fillers, the implants, the injections, the procedures "for themselves." And maybe they genuinely believe that. But it is impossible to separate our desires from the system that shaped those desires.

This is not about shaming women for their choices. Women have every right to do what they want with their own bodies. What matters is recognising the water we are all swimming in.

It's also true that men face appearance pressures of their own. You're told to be tall, lean, muscular, strong but not too bulky, rugged but not unkempt, attractive but effortlessly so - never trying too hard. Men aren't immune to insecurity. You feel the sting of comparison, too. The difference is scale, not existence. Women are drowning in it; men are swimming in the shallows. Recognising this isn't about minimising your experience. It's about understanding the weight is distributed unevenly, not exclusively.

Women are taught from childhood that beauty is currency. Good looks improve your chances.

Good looks increase your value.

Good looks make you worthy of attention, love and respect. No one says this out loud. They do not have to. Society delivers the message in a thousand smaller ways.

The thing many men do not fully grasp is that beauty standards do not only harm women. They harm men, too, just in a different direction.

Men are conditioned to believe that women exist for visual consumption. Not because men are innately objectifying, but because this is the story they have been fed since childhood. Think about mainstream media. In movies, books, ads and television, the male character is almost always dressed appropriately for the setting. He is an archaeologist in dusty clothing. A detective in a rumpled suit. A tradesman in worn work boots.

The female equivalent, however, is often dressed as though she accidentally wandered in from a photoshoot. The archaeologist has glossy hair, tight shorts and cleavage on display while exploring ruins. The firefighter has perfectly contoured cheeks while running into burning buildings. The soldier has time to curl her hair before combat. Even women in disaster films are rarely sweaty or dirty unless it is a plot point to make them look sexy in distress.

This is not coincidence. It is conditioning.
It sends a message to men and boys:
A woman's function is to be looked at.

Not to survive.
Not to lead.
Not to achieve.

Not to drive the plot.
To *decorate* it.

Men grow up consuming these images without questioning them. Then they hit adulthood and genuinely believe that a real partner should somehow meet the standard of a character designed by a male screenwriter and a makeup team.

The result is devastating for everyone.

Men struggle to connect with real women because real women look like human beings, not filtered fantasies. Women struggle to feel desirable because they believe they must live up to an impossible benchmark.
No one wins.

I cannot count the number of times women have told me they altered their bodies because they believed men would find them more attractive. Not because a man directly asked them to, but because the entire culture taught them that the male gaze is the ultimate judge of female worth.

Then, when women become frustrated and vocal about this system, men often assume they must hate men. Not at all. What women hate is the exhausting expectation that every part of their appearance should be optimised.

It is not that women do not enjoy beauty or self-expression. Many do. Creatively. Joyfully. Confidently. Fashion, makeup and styling can be forms of art, rebellion, identity and celebration.

The issue is not self-expression.
The issue is *obligation*.
There is a big difference between "I enjoy this," and "I must do this to be acceptable."
Most women land somewhere between the two. Men rarely see the toll because they are not expected to carry that weight.

A man can age without shame.
A man can gain weight without social punishment.
A man can have body hair without scrutiny.
A man can have wrinkles without being told to "fix" his face.
A man can be plain-looking without having his value questioned.

IF BEAUTY IS **CURRENCY**, WE NEED TO STOP FUELLING THE ECONOMY.

A woman, however, is expected to present herself as though she has a whole production team in her bathroom each morning.

Beauty standards, while targeted at women, have quietly harmed men as well, particularly younger men. Boys and teenagers have grown up with constant exposure to pornified imagery of women shaped entirely around male fantasy.

This creates a dangerous loop.

Women feel pressure to look like porn.
Men expect sex to look like porn.
Women feel pressure to perform like porn.
Men become desensitised to real women.

This is contributing to a rise in erectile dysfunction among teenage boys and men in their early twenties. Not because they are unhealthy, but because their brains have been conditioned to respond to artificial stimulation rather than the presence of a living, imperfect, beautiful human being.

Real women have cellulite.
Real women have skin texture.
Real women have stomach rolls when they sit.
Real women do not have permanent lighting or filters.
Real women do not walk around with permanently arched backs, glossy lips and perfectly positioned hair.

Men are not being unkind when they struggle to adjust. They have been trained from childhood to expect women to look like characters, not people.

Undoing this conditioning benefits men just as much as women. It reconnects men with reality. With intimacy. With emotional connection. With genuine desire rather than performance-based arousal.

Another layer worth exploring is how beauty standards shape women's behaviour beyond their physical appearance. Women are taught to be decorative. Pleasant. Pretty. Soft. Approachable. Non-threatening. The expectation of beauty bleeds into expectations of personality.

A woman who does not smile is rude.
A woman who does not flirt back is arrogant.
A woman who is not polite is hostile.
A woman who does not soften her tone is unfeminine.

The beauty standard does not just shape faces. It shapes behaviour. It teaches women that their social survival depends on their appearance and emotional appeal to others. That is a heavy load to carry.

Men are rarely taught this. Men are taught to lead, to speak, to dominate conversation, to take up space. Women are taught to shrink, physically and emotionally.

When women push back, when they refuse to be decorative, when they prioritise their capabilities over their appearance, they are often labelled difficult, aggressive or unfriendly. Men take it personally. They think she is rejecting them. In reality, she is rejecting the expectation that she exists for male comfort.

When women are told their worth lies in their appearance, men begin to subconsciously believe that women owe them beauty. They believe women owe them visual pleasure. They believe their preferences should guide women's choices.

This is why so many women experience unsolicited commentary about their bodies.

"You looked better before."
"Why would you cut your hair?"
"Men prefer natural beauty."

"Men like curves."
"Men like thinner women."
"Men don't like tattoos."
"Men love long hair."

Women receive endless advice about what men like, as though they exist to please an imaginary panel of male judges. It is exhausting. And it reinforces the idea that a woman's body is not hers. That her appearance is public property.

When men alter their bodies, no one assumes they did it for women. When men change their appearance, no one expects women to weigh in with approval or disapproval. Men's bodies belong to them. Women's bodies are treated as communal conversation pieces.

Here is what men need to know: women do not expect perfection from men. Women do not expect men to change their entire relationship with beauty overnight. What women want is understanding. Awareness. Empathy. Recognition.

Women want men to understand that beauty standards are not superficial issues. They shape careers. Confidence. Self-worth. Relationships. Sexuality. Mental health. Safety. Everything.

Women want men to stop assuming beauty is for them.
Women want men to stop comparing real women to fictional ones.
Women want men to see the pressure, not the result.
Women want men to value capability over appearance.
Women want men to love them in ways that have nothing to do with aesthetics.

Most importantly, women want men to see them as whole people, not as visual assets.

Let me return to my daughter for a moment.

People comment on her beauty constantly. They love her curls, her eyes, her cheeks, the way she swans around like she owns every room she enters. And yes, she is beautiful.

But here is what unsettles me.
Her beauty is the first thing people see.
Her beauty is the first thing people comment on.
Her beauty is what the world praises.

And she has so much more to offer than that.

She is bold. She is stubborn. She is curious. She is brave in a way that startles me. She problem-solves like she is in training for a future heist. She has a spark in her, capable of lighting a fire that deserves to be named.

But when the world keeps calling her beautiful before it calls her skilled, she learns that is where her value lies.

It does not worry me that she is beautiful, but that beauty will try to become her entire identity. That she will begin to believe her worth rises and falls with her appearance. That she will mistake admiration for validation. That the world will convince her that the face she sees in the mirror is more important than the mind, strength and spirit that live behind it.

She deserves better than that.
All girls do.
All women do.
And this is where men come in.

Men have the power to disrupt the beauty-first narrative simply by choosing to see women fully. When men praise intelligence, humour, talent, courage, and strength with the same enthusiasm they praise beauty, they help reshape what women learn about their worth. When men stop treating appearance as currency, they help destabilise the system that taught women to invest everything they have into being visually acceptable.

This is not about rejecting beauty. Beauty can be joyful. Beauty can be expressive. Beauty can be fun. But beauty becomes the beast when it becomes the measure of a woman's value.

Beauty becomes the beast when women are taught it is the most important thing they can offer.
Beauty becomes the beast when girls grow up believing their power lies in how they look rather than who they are.
Beauty becomes the beast when men only learn to notice the surface.
Beauty becomes the beast when women are punished for aging, changing or existing outside unrealistic standards.

The danger was never beauty itself.
The danger is the weight the world puts on it.

When men understand that, when they see how deeply this system cuts, everything shifts. Women stop feeling trapped by appearance. Men stop feeling confused by women's insecurities. Relationships become more equal. Attraction becomes more real. And girls like my daughter grow up knowing they are more than what strangers see at first glance.

Beauty may be admired.
But it should never be the foundation of a human being's worth.

That is the beast we are trying to slay.

Think about the compliments you tend to give girls and women. Are they mostly about looks? Fair enough - we've all been taught to notice the outside first. But what might you see if you paid attention to what she says, does, or thinks instead? What changes when you widen the lens?

CHAPTER SEVEN
Private Property

A reality check on safety, vigilance, and everyday calculations.

By trade, I currently work in the wedding industry. I have photographed hundreds of weddings, which means I have spent years standing on the outskirts of large, energetic groups of people as they become progressively more intoxicated. I am stone sober the entire time, camera in hand, watching everything unfold with the clarity that only sobriety provides while everyone else drifts steadily into chaos.

It is in this setting that I have seen a particular pattern repeat itself again and again. As the drinks flow, the music gets louder, and inhibitions loosen, the behaviour of some men begins to shift. Their jokes get bolder. Their comments get flirtier. Their boundaries get blurrier. And the line between playful banter and inappropriate behaviour becomes dangerously thin.

This is not theoretical. It is lived.

At a recent wedding, there was an older man, maybe late fifties or early sixties, who started the day with harmless jokes. A few lighthearted comments. Nothing rude or inappropriate. He was the cheerful, slightly cheeky uncle type. I brushed it off as part of the job. If you work in weddings long enough, you become an expert at smiling politely while dodging weird humour from guests you will never see again.

But as the evening progressed and the alcohol kept coming, the dynamic shifted. His jokes came with a hand on my arm. Then a hand on my lower back. The laughter became paired with lingering touches. The final straw came when his hand slid around my hip and pulled me toward him, planting a kiss on my cheek, which only landed there because I swiftly turned my lips away.

I did not consent to it. I did not want it. I did not invite it. I did not feel flattered. I felt trapped while at work, expected to laugh it off because men like him are considered "harmless". Reacting honestly—calling it out as the sexual assault that it was—would have me labelled as overreactive or unprofessional long before anyone acknowledges that the man crossed a boundary.

The comments were harmless. The entitlement was not. He wanted access to my body because he felt comfortable, because he was drunk, because the culture allowed him to think it was acceptable. And I was expected to protect his dignity more than my comfort.

If you are a man reading this, ask yourself honestly: would you brush it off so quickly if an unknown older man slid an arm around your hip, pulled you in and pressed his lips to your face without your permission?

Would you view it as friendly?
Harmless?
A compliment?

Of course not.
So, why should I?

This incident was not unique. It was not shocking. It was routine. Throughout my twenties, particularly during my bar-hopping, dancing, living-my-best-reckless-social-life era, my body was treated like public property every single time I entered a crowded venue. Strange hands on my hips. Passing hands on my backside. A stranger's arm around my waist. Men leaning in too close, breathing into my neck as if proximity itself was permission.

If you ask any woman you know, she will tell you the same story. Not once or twice. Hundreds of times. It is so common that women began treating it as an unavoidable part of nightlife, like overpriced drinks or sticky floors. We normalised it because we were expected to. The alternative was to be labelled dramatic, difficult, or a killjoy.

This is the root of the problem. Women are raised to swallow discomfort to protect male feelings. Men are raised to believe their desire to touch is innocent, even flattering. Both groups are taught these roles so early and consistently that, by adulthood, the pattern feels natural.

It is not natural.
It is learned.

One of the most persistent and dangerous myths men internalise is the belief that they are entitled to women's bodies in small ways. Not outright ownership. Not violent control. Just minor claims. A hand on the waist to get past her. A touch on the lower back to guide her through a doorway. A hug she did not initiate. A kiss on the cheek she did not ask for. A hand on her thigh because she "did not move away." A stare that lingers far too long.

None of these things seems violent. None seems abusive. None seems worth calling out. And that is precisely why they are so insidious.

The problem is not the physical sensation of a hand. The problem is in the message beneath it.

The message says:
I am allowed to touch you.
Your comfort is secondary.

Your boundaries must bend around mine.
Your body exists in part for my access.

Women do not fear the hand itself.
Women fear what the hand represents.

Because every minor violation that is brushed aside makes room for larger ones. Every time a woman is expected to accept an unwanted touch because "he meant well," she learns her boundaries will not be respected unless she defends them aggressively. And if she defends them aggressively, *she* becomes the problem.

Men get to label their behaviour by their intention.
Women are judged by how willing they are to tolerate it.

Let me speak frankly: entitlement does not begin with violence. It begins with familiarity.

A man who grabs a woman's hip in a bar without asking is not trying to assault her. But he is acting on the belief that he is allowed to initiate that level of physical intimacy without thinking about her comfort.

He does not have to consider whether it will frighten her.
He does not have to consider whether she wants it.
He does not have to consider whether she feels safe.
He only has to consider whether he feels like doing it.

This is the imbalance women feel every day. The weight of knowing that men can touch them casually, thoughtlessly, without consequence. The weight of knowing that the world sees those touches as harmless and sees women's discomfort as excessive.

Men are allowed to misjudge.
Women are not allowed to object.

Before anyone raises the predictable objection, let me acknowledge something. Yes, sometimes women touch men without permission. Yes, some men experience unwanted touching. This is real and valid. But it is not symmetrical. It is not culturally normalised for women to touch men freely. It is not seen as flattering for women to grab men in bars. Society does not tell men they should feel grateful for the attention.

Women are told they should take it as a compliment.
Men are told they should take it as a warning.

The stakes are not equal.
The risks are not equal.
The cultural messaging is not equal.

Women touching men without permission or invitation is still unacceptable. If a man feels unsafe, threatened or disrespected by unwanted physical contact, that experience is valid. The point is not to dismiss men's discomfort or pretend it does not matter. It does.
But using those situations to minimise the far more frequent, culturally normalised pattern of men touching women is not the solution. One does not cancel out the other. These are two separate issues, both worth addressing and taking seriously. Acknowledging the impact on women does not diminish the effect on men, and recognising the impact on men does not erase the impact on women. They can coexist. They should coexist. And both deserve thoughtful, honest attention.

The most pervasive form of entitlement manifests in how men interpret rejection. When a woman pulls away, steps back or freezes, many men read it as shyness rather than refusal. When a woman does not laugh, men assume she is uptight rather than uncomfortable. When a woman says no subtly, men treat it as a soft yes.

Women often describe the moment unwanted touch happens as a split-second freeze. Their bodies lock up, their brains

CONTROL DOESN'T NEED VIOLENCE.
IT JUST NEEDS A CULTURE THAT STAYS QUIET.

short-circuit, and they stay completely still while they figure out what level of danger they are in. Men interpret this stillness as permission.

This is why the idea of "friendly" touch becomes complicated. What feels friendly to a man can feel threatening to a woman depending on her history, the context and the power dynamic. A woman does not need to cry or shout for a boundary to be crossed. Her discomfort is enough. But discomfort is rarely taken seriously unless it is *loud*.

Women are conditioned to minimise.
Men are conditioned to assume.

This is not a personal flaw in men. It is a systemic misunderstanding built over generations.

To understand why women react so strongly to boundary violations that seem small to men, you must understand the background noise women live with. Women walk through the world with a constant emotional checklist. Around 70% of women change their routes, routines, or behaviour for safety reasons. It shows up with thoughts like;

Is this man looking at me?
Is it friendly or assessing?
Is he following too close?
Are the exits visible?
Is there someone near enough to intervene?
Should I send my location to a friend?
Should I pretend to answer a call?
Should I take the long way home?

Men rarely have to think like this. Women think like this every day.

So, when a man touches a woman without permission, even lightly, even playfully, she feels the entire weight of that vigilance in her body. She feels powerless because she has learned over and over that saying "stop" can escalate rather than resolve.

Understanding this is not about guilt. It is about empathy.

There is another layer that often gets overlooked. Women who experience boundary violations at work frequently feel even more trapped than in social spaces. A workplace touch is not just unwanted; it is dangerous. Calling it out can threaten a woman's job, reputation or safety. Ignoring it can invite more.

In my job as a photographer, I often cannot react the way I want to. My safety, professionalism and livelihood depend on my ability to absorb discomfort without escalating the situation. If I push back, I risk being perceived as unprofessional. If I say nothing, I risk reinforcing the behaviour.

This is the impossible position women are constantly in.

Women are punished for speaking up.
Women are punished for staying silent.
Women carry the responsibility for managing men's behaviour.
Men carry the privilege of assuming their behaviour is harmless.

And the cycle continues.

Men do not need to see themselves as predators to understand why these small moments matter. Most men would never harm a woman. Most men do not intend to intimidate, frighten or disrespect anyone. But intention does not erase impact. And impact is what women feel.

If you are a man reading this, I want to offer something important. Women do not expect you to apologise for other men's behaviour. Women do not expect you never to touch anyone again. Women are not accusing all men of entitlement.

Women want you to understand the system so you can move through the world without unconsciously reinforcing it.
Women want you to be aware.
Women want you to be observant.
Women want you to recognise discomfort rather than dismiss it.
Women want you to notice power dynamics in a room.
Women want you to understand that small touches carry big messages.

This awareness is not difficult. It is not political. It is not radical.

Women do not want to be protected. They want to be respected. They want autonomy over their bodies. They want their boundaries understood by default, not defended at high cost. They want men to see that physical contact is not neutral for everyone.

If men can understand that, genuinely understand it, these moments will change. The culture will shift. Women will feel safer. Men will feel less confused by women's reactions. Boundaries will become clearer and respected without resentment.

Women are not fragile. Women are not overreacting. Women are not dramatic. They are navigating a world that taught men to assume access to their bodies.

Men can help change that dynamic simply by becoming conscious of it.

Your touch is not inherently dangerous.
But a woman's comfort is inherently important.

Picture yourself walking into a crowded pub and having to stay slightly on guard the whole time. Not paranoid - just switched on. What would you want from the men around you if that were your everyday reality?

When a man considers that, everything that follows becomes safer.

For him.
For her.
For everyone.

CHAPTER EIGHT

The #NotAllMen Reflex

Why defending yourself derails the conversation — even if you mean well.

Did you know that if you search "protective equipment for men" online, the results are exactly what you would expect. Hard hats. Steel cap boots. High-visibility gear. Face shields. Ear protection. Tools and equipment designed to protect a man from workplace hazards. Practical, logical, sensible.

Now search "protective equipment for women."

Suddenly, the results shift from workplace safety to personal survival. Alarms. Pepper spray. Keychain weapons. Hidden blades. Whistles. Emergency apps. Self-defence classes.

Advice pages on how to avoid being attacked while walking to your car at night. Entire catalogues dedicated to preventing violence.

When it comes to men, protection is optional and task-based. When it comes to women, protection is constant and survival-based.

Women do not see these results and think, "What a clever algorithm." Women see these results and think, "Yes. That tracks."

This is the world we live in. A world where products for men assume danger is occasional and innocent, and products for women assume danger is daily and malicious.

This is why the phrase "Not all men" hits the way it does. It is technically accurate. Not all men behave violently. Not all men harass women. Not all men assault, belittle or intimidate. Most men consider themselves good men. Most men would never dream of hurting a woman.

But here is the part men rarely realise.

Women *know* that.
Women have *always* known that.

Women know it is not all men. Like I said earlier, the frustration is that too many men think that saying this is helpful, when all it does is change the subject from women's safety to men's feelings.

"Not all men" turns a woman's experience into a man's reassurance.
It derails the conversation.
It redirects the focus.
It responds to fear with defensiveness rather than empathy.

And the more men insist on saying it, the more it feels like they care more about defending themselves from an implication that was never directed at them, than the safety of another human being.

Let's talk about perspective.
This isn't just personal experience - the numbers tell the same story, over and over.

One in five women has survived sexual violence.
97% of young women report experiencing harassment from men in their lives.
One in six women has been stalked.
One third have been physically assaulted.
And in Australia, a woman is killed by a partner every fourteen days.

These aren't edge cases or dramatic outliers. They're the backdrop of women's lives.

So when women talk about harassment, coercion, stalking, or violence, they're not talking about the average man. They're talking about the experiences that shaped their entire understanding of safety.

Imagine a woman walking alone at night. She hears footsteps behind her. She cannot see who it is. She cannot assess intent. She cannot determine risk. She has to react based on possibility, not certainty.

She is not thinking, "That man is dangerous."
She is thinking, "I cannot afford to guess wrong."

Women's fear is not about individual men.
It is about the statistical reality that men commit 90% of violence against women.

This is not about blame.
This is about probability.

Most men are safe.
But most perpetrators are men.

Women navigate that contradiction every day.

The emotional disconnect here is profound.

When men hear, "Men scare women," they often interpret it as a personal insult.
When women say, "Men scare us," they are stating a lived truth.

Men hear accusation.
Women are expressing caution.

Men hear, "You are dangerous."

Women mean, "I cannot tell who is safe."

Men hear blame.
Women are sharing survival strategies.

This is why "Not all men" feels dismissive. It is not an answer to the problem women are raising. It is an interruption that tries to comfort men rather than protect women.

It centres men in a conversation where men are not the ones at risk.

One of the hardest things for some men to accept is that women do not have the luxury of assessing men as individuals until safety is established. A woman cannot wait until she knows a man well before deciding whether she needs to protect herself from him. Her brain makes that assessment within seconds based on context, body language, tone and instinct.

Men often say, "Give us a chance."
Women are thinking, "I will. But first, I need to stay alive."

It sounds dramatic if you are a man who has never feared bodily harm from the opposite sex. It is not dramatic for women. It is normal. It is rational. It is ingrained.

Let me illustrate the scale of this.

Every woman you know has been followed, harassed, hit on aggressively, touched without permission or spoken to in a way that made her deeply uncomfortable. Not occasionally. Persistently.

Women do not share the full extent with men because they know how often men respond with minimising comments.
"It was just a compliment."
"He probably didn't mean it."
"You should take it as flattery."

#NOTALLMEN
IS TRUE IN THE SAME WAY
'NOT ALL GUNS ARE LOADED'
IS TRUE.
IT STILL MEANS NO-ONE CAN
SAFELY PULL A TRIGGER.

"You're overreacting."
"Not all men are like that."

None of these statements makes the situation safer. They simply teach women that sharing their experiences is an emotional burden to men.

So, women stop sharing.
They stop explaining.
They stop trusting that men can hear the truth without thinking it is an attack.

This silence is not progress. It is exhaustion.

There is another layer here that deserves attention. When men say, "Not all men," what they often mean is, "I am not like that." They are trying to say, "I care," "I am safe," "I would protect you," "I am one of the good ones."

And that is a wonderful instinct.
It comes from a desire to be trusted.
But trust is not built through denial.
Trust is built through understanding.

You do not prove you are safe by insisting women should feel safe around you. You prove you are safe by acknowledging why they do not.

The phrase "Not all men" attempts to distance a good man from bad behaviour. The human ego is wired this way. It wants to protect itself. It wants to be seen as good. It wants to be separate from wrongdoing.

But this is not about individual identity. It is about cultural responsibility.
Men are not being blamed for existing.
Men are being asked to recognise the environment in which women exist.

Men did not create the system.
But men have enormous influence over how it operates.

Every time a man listens without defensiveness, calls out harmful behaviour, teaches his sons respect, intervenes when a friend crosses a line, or supports a woman's boundaries, he becomes part of the solution.

Every time a man says, "Not all men," he becomes part of the stall.
A better approach is to ask, "How can I be part of reducing the risk?"

One is defensive.
One is proactive.

Let me make one thing absolutely clear.
This is not about vilifying men.
This is about contextualising women's fear.

Most men are not dangerous.
But almost all women have encountered men who were.

Most men would never harm a woman.
But almost all women know someone who has been harmed.

When men insist, "Not all men," they are technically correct, but emotionally out of step.
Correct in fact.
Incorrect in context.

Women know not all men.
Women also know too many men.

There is a powerful shift that happens when men stop trying to separate themselves from the problem and instead say, "I understand why you feel this way." That sentence alone changes the entire dynamic.

If you are a man reading this, here is the most honest truth I can give you:

The women in your life likely already know you are not "that" man.
What they need is for you to show other men not to be "that" man either.

Not through violence or confrontation, but through influence, modelling, interrupting harmful behaviour, setting standards for your male friends, and raising boys who understand boundaries and empathy.

"Not all men" stops the conversation.
"I hear you" moves it forward.

There is one final layer here, and it might be the most important.

When women talk about danger, what they are actually describing is power. The imbalance of it. The unpredictability of it. The consequences of it.

Men do not fear women the way women fear men because men do not live in a world where women routinely overpower, intimidate or violate them. Women do not have cultural permission to harm men. Men do have that permission.

This is not because men are inherently violent.
This is because men have historically been granted more physical, social and legal power.

Women are not saying men are dangerous.
Women are saying men are powerful.

"Not all men" may be true.
But "enough men" is also true.

And until the gap between those two truths closes, women will continue to speak up.

Not to blame you.
To survive you.
To trust you.
To hope you will join them.

So, next time your gut reaction is, "Yeah, but I'm not like that," hit pause. Ask yourself what you're actually trying to protect - your ego, or the chance to understand someone else's experience? What happens if, just once, you sit with the comment instead of distancing yourself from it?

CHAPTER NINE
I'm Sorry, We're Done
A look at repair, accountability, and what actually rebuilds trust.

A while ago, I was arguing with my husband about something that genuinely mattered to me. Not one of those surface arguments about towels on the floor or whether he put the pots away in the wrong cupboard again. This had emotional weight. I was trying to explain why something hurt, what it triggered in me, and why I needed him to understand rather than brush it off.

Halfway through my sentence, he said, "I'm sorry."

And then he sat back as if a referee had blown a whistle. Argument over. Game finished. Problem solved.

Except nothing was solved. He apologised in the same way someone would press the silence button on a smoke alarm. The noise stops, but the fire is still active.

I kept talking.
He looked confused.
In his mind, we were already done.

"What more do you want from me?" he asked.
"I said sorry."

I wanted him to understand.
I wanted him to hear me.
I wanted him to stay in the discomfort long enough to connect the dots between what happened and why it affected me.

He thought the apology was the full stop.

I needed it to be the comma.

He was not trying to be dismissive.
He genuinely believed the apology fixed the emotional problem.

To him, the job was complete.
To me, the repair had barely begun.

That moment was a tiny window into one of the most significant divides between men and women. Men often believe they are resolving a conflict by ending it. Women often believe conflict is resolved when they feel understood.

It is not the same thing at all.

Emotional safety is not a mystical concept. It is not spiritual alignment, and it doesn't require crystals or a sound bath. It is far more straightforward and far more practical.

Emotional safety means you can express what you feel without bracing for impact.
It means your emotions will not be dismissed as silly or exaggerated.
It means your partner will not treat vulnerability like a personal attack.
It means you can tell the truth without worrying that the truth will be used against you later.

It is the sense that your relationship can withstand reality.

Women know instantly whether emotional safety is present. Men often assume it is there because they are not actively shouting. But silence is not safety. Calm is not safety. Politeness is not safety. Safety is felt, not declared.

Men sometimes measure emotional safety by what they *do not*

do:
"I don't yell."
"I don't insult her."
"I don't stonewall for hours."

Women measure emotional safety by what they *can* do:
Can I speak without shrinking myself?
Can I express disappointment without punishment?
Can I be emotional without being treated like an inconvenience?
Can I tell the truth without losing closeness?

This is why emotional safety matters.
It is the invisible glue that holds intimacy, trust and communication together.

Without it, everything becomes performative.
With it, everything becomes possible.

One of the biggest reasons men accidentally undermine emotional safety is that many of them were raised to believe emotions are problems to be solved, not experiences to be shared.

Women tend to approach conflict like a conversation.
Men tend to approach conflict like a roof leak.

Find the source.
Patch it quickly.
Declare the crisis resolved.
Go back to watching TV.

Women want to talk through the emotional landscape.
Men want to restore structural stability so they can sit down again.

And honestly, it would be adorable if it didn't create so many issues.

Men apologise fast because they think that ends the discomfort.
Women need the discomfort to be understood before it dissolves.

Men hear emotions and think "solution."
Women express emotions looking for connection.

Men want to end the argument.
Women want to understand each other.

His focus is on closure.
Her focus is on repair.

There are specific phrases men say during conflict that feel harmless to them but drop through a woman's body like an elevator plunging down a shaft.

"It wasn't that big of a deal."
"It was a joke."
"You're being too sensitive."
"I didn't mean it like that."
"You shouldn't feel that way."
"Can we not do this?"
"You're overreacting."
"Let it go."

Men do not say these things because they want to hurt women.
They say them because they want the moment to stop being uncomfortable.

They want to return to emotional equilibrium.
They want to go back to feeling like everything is fine.

The problem is simple.
These phrases do not soothe women.
They suffocate them.
Minimising someone's emotional experience does not calm

AN APOLOGY WITHOUT BEHAVIOURAL CHANGE IS NOT SINCERITY. IT'S STRATEGY.

them down.
It makes them feel unseen, unheard, and alone within the relationship.

And here is the part men rarely admit out loud:
These phrases are often panic responses.

A woman says, "This hurt me," and a man hears, "You failed."
He hears, "You are the problem."
He hears, "You are not good enough."

So, he shifts emotional gears into self-protection mode and tries to end the conversation quickly. Not because he does not care about her emotions, but because he does not know what to do with them.

The conflict is not actually between him and her.
It is between him and his own fear.
Fear of being inadequate.
Fear of being the villain.
Fear of being unable to fix it.
Fear of being emotionally exposed.

Emotional safety collapses right there, in that split second where she needs him to stay open, and he closes up.

And yet he is not wrong for feeling overwhelmed.
He is human.
He was never taught how to handle emotional depth without sprinting toward the exit. And this is where the system built *for* men starts to *fail* men. Because emotional safety benefits men just as much as women. Sometimes even more.

Men in emotionally safe relationships:
Communicate better.
Feel more respected.
Feel more desired.
Have more sex.

Fight less.
Recover faster.
Stay more connected.
Feel more confident.
Experience deeper trust.
Stop walking around on emotional autopilot.

Men think emotional safety is something they *give*.
They rarely realise it is also something they *receive*.

A woman who feels emotionally safe becomes softer, more affectionate, open, warm, sexual, trusting, and generous. Not because she is performing for him, but because she no longer needs to guard herself.

When a woman does not feel safe, she becomes guarded.
When a woman feels safe, she becomes expansive.

Women often feel emotionally unsafe long before a relationship becomes visibly strained. They feel it in quiet ways.

They feel it when their feelings are brushed aside.
They feel it when they are told not to take something personally.
They feel it when a man's discomfort takes priority over their pain.
They feel it when they cannot predict whether being honest will bring closeness or conflict.
They feel it when expressing a need results in anger and an argument rather than understanding.

Women stop sharing not because they lack emotions but because they lack safety.

Men rarely realise this is happening. From their perspective, things seem peaceful. Fewer arguments. Fewer emotional conversations. Fewer tense moments.

From her perspective, things seem lonely.

She is not *feeling* less.
She is simply *saying* less.

Silence is not peace.
Silence is self-protection.

And once emotional silence settles in, relationships start to die from the inside out.

Men sometimes avoid emotional conversations because they fear making things worse. They fear saying the wrong thing. They fear the spiral of emotions they do not know how to fix. They fear being seen as the cause of the distress.

So, they shut down to avoid the sensation of failure.

Women interpret the shutdown as rejection.

He is retreating because he cares.
She feels abandoned because she cares.

Both are hurting for the same reason.
Both are protecting themselves.
Both are longing for connection.
Neither is getting it.

If men could see how much power they have to soothe the woman they love simply by staying open for five more minutes, they would never underestimate the importance of emotional safety again.

To create emotional safety, men do not need to become different people.
They need to become more *available* people.

Men often underestimate how deeply women crave presence.

Not solutions.
Not perfect words.
Not therapy sessions.
Presence.

Women want to feel that their emotions do not chase men away.
That their feelings are not a burden.
That their vulnerability is welcome.
That the man they love can stand beside them in the mess, not just the calm.

They do not want to be rescued from their emotions.
They want to be held through them.

Not physically, although that helps.
Emotionally.
Attentively.
With interest, not reluctance.

Think of a time you apologised, but it didn't land. What were you really aiming for - making things right or getting the heat off you? If you replayed that moment now, what would you do differently? What would you listen for that you may have missed the first time?

CHAPTER TEN
Communication, not Combat
The habits that turn discussions into standoffs.

A friend once told me about a fight with her partner that started as an honest conversation and turned into something entirely different.

She had approached him calmly.
Genuinely calmly.
Not "woman saying she's calm but actually vibrating with fury," calm.
Actual calm.

She said, "It hurt me when you told that story about me in front of your friends. I felt embarrassed."

This is a clear sentence.
A plain sentence.
Not coded.
Not dramatic.
Not laced with secret meaning.

But instead of addressing the part about him, he swivelled and laser-focused on the part about her.

"Why are you so sensitive about everything?" he asked.

And just like that, the entire conversation left the runway and crash-landed in a field of resentment.

Her hurt was no longer the topic.
Her sensitivity was.

She tried again.
"It's not being sensitive. I just didn't enjoy being the punchline."

He sighed dramatically; the kind of sigh that said, "Here we go again".
"I'm not responsible for how you take things," he said.

Again, we see the maneuver.
She was talking about his behaviour.
He was talking about her interpretation.

Within three minutes, the original issue was gone.
Extinct.
Dead.
Buried under a pile of conversational distractions.

He began questioning her tone.
Then her timing.
Then her logic.
Then her "habit of overreacting."
Then, whether she was projecting.
Then, whether she had slept enough lately.
Then, whether she was "going to start bleeding tomorrow".

At one point, he genuinely said, "I think your feelings are confusing the facts." As if her emotional experience were a rogue witness who should be escorted out of the courtroom.

By the end of the discussion, she found herself apologising for being upset.

Not because she was wrong. But because the entire conversation had been co-opted, reframed, and weaponised into something she never initiated.

That is deflection.
That is conversational misdirection.
That is communication used as a shield rather than a bridge.

Communication problems in relationships are rarely about complicated topics.
They are about strategy.
They are about learned conversational habits that men do not realise they use, and women do not know how to dismantle without sounding "emotional," which then feeds the cycle again.

This isn't to say women never use unhealthy communication strategies. Of course they do. Everyone does at times. What I'm pointing to here is a pattern I see and hear about repeatedly in men's communication with women - a pattern shaped by social conditioning, not personal flaw. Naming that pattern doesn't erase women's missteps; it simply highlights a dynamic that shows up consistently in heterosexual relationships.
This chapter is not about getting men to talk more.
It is about getting men to talk differently.

With clarity.
With ownership.
With self-awareness.
With an understanding that "I don't understand" is not neutral when it is used as a conversational escape hatch.

Communication without combat is not about avoiding conflict.
It is about refusing to use communication as a competitive sport.

When a man hears, "That upset me," he often thinks, "I failed," and immediately shifts into either:
Defend
Deny
Debate
Distract
Or disassemble her argument word by word, like he is dismantling a bomb.

Men are not doing this because they do not care.

They are doing it because they do not know how to sit with the idea that their behaviour had a negative impact. When a man reacts with panic or defensiveness, it doesn't usually mean he's trying to be difficult. More often, it's the emotional equivalent of a muscle that was never allowed to grow. Men are raised to solve problems, not feel them. So, when a feeling shows up - especially one he doesn't have a name for - it hits like an alarm instead of information. That rush of heat or tightness in his chest isn't drama. It's overwhelm. He was never taught how to hold that emotion, only how to silence it.

Men fear the accusation.
They fear being the bad guy.
They fear the feeling of being responsible for someone's pain, even unintentionally.

So instead of staying in the moment, they argue about the wording.
The delivery.
The timing.
The tone.
The expression.
The logic.
Anything except the behaviour itself.

Women feel like they are trying to talk about the plot, while men focus on picking apart the grammar.

Arguments feel different when one partner has been trained to watch for every structural weakness, and the other has been taught that the foundation is solid.

Many men underestimate how dominant their conversational habits are.
Not because men are rude, but because men are trained to speak in a way that preserves their internal stability rather than

the connection in the moment.

What this creates is a set of predictable, repeatable patterns.

A woman raises a point.
A man responds to her delivery instead of the point.
She tries to clarify.
He critiques the clarification.
She tries again.
He escalates with irritation.
She withdraws or intensifies.
He labels it as an overreaction.
She wonders why she ever attempted the conversation.

Everything gets discussed.
Except for the original issue.

This is communication turning into combat without anyone intending it.

A very subtle yet damaging habit is the linguistic pivot.
The art of shifting the spotlight from the topic to the tone.
It looks like this:

She says, "I was surprised by what you said."
He says, "Your tone is aggressive."

She says, "I didn't love how that came across."
He says, "You always jump to conclusions."

She says, "I want to talk about the way you spoke to me."
He says, "You can lose the attitude first."

Every time this happens, she is placed in the position of defending the way she requested clarity rather than discussing the behaviour that led her to raise it.

It is conversational whiplash.

A SYSTEM BUILT ON **DOMINANCE** PRODUCES CONVERSATIONS BUILT ON **DEFENCE** AND **DEFLECTION**.

It is the equivalent of someone saying, "My foot is stuck in the door," and the other person replied, "Well, you could have said that in a nicer tone."

Communication without combat starts with keeping the spotlight where it belongs.

Not on her pitch, her facial expressions or her sentence structure.
On the behaviour she brought up.

The moment a man debates delivery rather than substance, he is no longer communicating. He is negotiating the terms of engagement and is subtly but effectively dismantling trust and connection in his own relationship. It is self-sabotage thinly veiled as participation.

Communication without combat requires dismantling the subtle habits that turn discussions into battles.

One of the most common is the urge to win.

Men often fall into strategic debating without realising it.
They begin collecting supporting points like courtroom evidence.
They cross-examine her phrasing.
They point out inconsistencies.
They bring up previous examples that contradict her statement.
They latch onto the most minor detail she got wrong and inflate it into the main issue.

But conversations are not trials.
They're connectors.

Winning an argument is useless if the connection breaks.
Most women are not looking for victory.
They are looking for coherence.

They do not want a partner who crushes their statements with technical precision.
They want a partner who listens and responds to the topic as presented.

Men who argue to win usually lose something far more valuable: trust in their conversational presence.

Conversations are not a sport.
You are not trying to outscore your partner.
You are trying to understand each other well enough that the score no longer matters.

Speaking of keeping score, one of the most common derailments in relationships is what I call conversational time travel. She brings up something from this week. He responds by teleporting them to something she did yesterday, last month, last year, or in 2018, during a heated game of Catan.

She says, "The comment you made at dinner was unnecessary."
He says, "You make unnecessary comments all the time."

She says, "I didn't like how you shut me down earlier."
He says, "You do that too, you can't really talk."

She says, "I want to talk about how you handled that situation."
He says, "If we are comparing behaviour, let's talk about how you handled the situation yesterday."

This is not communication.
This is a defensive audit.

It is the conversational equivalent of dropping paperwork on the table and saying,
"Before we discuss my behaviour, let us discuss Exhibit B: The Time You Also Did Something."

Men do this because they believe that proving she is not

flawless somehow balances the scales.
As if two imperfect moments cancel each other out.
As if locating her past missteps reduces the current one.
As if equality of wrongdoing magically removes accountability.

It is a strange mathematical equation:
If she ever did anything remotely similar, he believes the current discussion becomes void.

But relationships are not algebra.
There is no cancelling out of variables.
Two wrongs do not neutralise each other at the conversational level.

All it does is make her wonder why she bothers raising anything at all. Don't get me wrong—I am not suggesting that her bad behaviour should not be raised and addressed through a constructive conversation... I am saying that this conversation is not the time, because you are not raising her wrongdoing to facilitate actual communication – you are deflecting.
It is avoidance disguised as logic.

It shifts the spotlight away from the issue she surfaced and shines it directly on her history, her imperfections, and her occasional off days.
Suddenly, the conversation becomes a scavenger hunt for evidence that she has also misstepped at some point.

Even worse, the catalogue of her past behaviour rarely aligns with the topic at hand.

She is trying to talk about apples.
He is responding with mangoes from three autumns ago.

And then he wonders why she looks frustrated.

The issue is not that he sees patterns.
The issue is that he uses them as shields instead of mirrors.

A healthy conversation says,
"I hear what you're raising. Let me look at that."

Deflection says,
"I hear what you're raising, but here is something you once did, so let us focus on that instead."

Deflection gives the illusion of contribution while actually contributing nothing to the topic.
It swaps accountability for comparison.
It swaps curiosity for competition.
It swaps dialogue for distraction.

And worst of all, it teaches her that bringing anything up will cause a courtroom analysis of her conduct rather than a discussion of his.

Over time, she stops raising concerns at all, not because she has none, but because she has learned that every single conversation will be turned around and handed back to her like a boomerang.

Communication without combat is the opposite of time travel.

It stays in the moment.
It stays in this event.
It stays with the point as raised.
It acknowledges what she surfaced without immediately scanning her history for leverage.

When a man can resist the urge to deflect, everything changes.
The argument shortens.
The tone softens.
The trust strengthens.
The entire conversation becomes cleaner, calmer and more productive.

She no longer has to battle for the right to raise an issue.

And he no longer has to catalogue her history to survive the topic.

We've all had arguments where we jumped in too quick, talked over the point, or defended ourselves before actually hearing the other person. Think of the last time you did that. What were you scared of losing - control, pride, the upper hand? What might happen if you slowed down and actually listened first?

CHAPTER ELEVEN
The Myth of Masculinity
Where the myths come from, and why they're worth challenging.

A few years ago, I was at a wedding where the groom spent the entire morning pretending he wasn't nervous. He was pale. Sweaty. Breathing like someone who had just sprinted uphill with a piano strapped to his back. He could barely get his tie on. His best man kept giving him water. His mum was secretly blotting his forehead every time he looked away.

Everyone could see it.
Everyone knew he was on the brink of panic.
Everyone understood that weddings are a pressure cooker for men.

But every time someone asked if he was alright, he said, "I'm good."
Every time someone offered help, he said, "I've got it."
Every time someone suggested he take a minute to breathe, he said, "I don't need to."

He walked around with the posture of someone trying to hold a building up with his spinal cord, insisting everything was fine while his hands shook so badly, he nearly stabbed himself with his cufflink.

At one point, the celebrant, bless her, gently suggested that nerves were absolutely normal.

He laughed it off as if it were the most ridiculous idea in the world.

Later, after the ceremony, after the vows, after the photos, after the speeches, after the whiskey, and after he finally relaxed enough to let the blood return to his face, he admitted quietly that he had been terrified.

Human emotion.
Normal stress.
An entirely reasonable response to a huge life event.
All denied because he had been taught that masculinity requires armour, not honesty.

The system did that.
Not biology.
A system that hands men a script so narrow they sometimes forget they were born with a full range of human wiring.

My story isn't the point - it's just one doorway into a much bigger pattern.

Masculinity, as most men inherited it, is not a natural identity.
It is a performance.
A very demanding one.

And it is time to retire it.

Men often hear conversations about patriarchy and think it is an attack on them.
It is not.
The system hurts men, too.
Deeply.
Silently.
Consistently.

It teaches boys to suppress half of their personality.
It teaches young men to translate vulnerability into silence.
It teaches grown men to carry pressure on their own.
It teaches partners to mistake emotional shutdown for strength.

It teaches fathers to love quietly instead of loudly.
It teaches husbands to hide their internal world because showing it is dangerous, unmanly or embarrassing.

The system is not a conspiracy.
It is a cultural blueprint that has been photocopied through generations.

And what passes for masculinity today is not strength.
It is restriction.

Men have been sold a counterfeit version of manhood.
A version that glorifies stoicism, dominance, control, detachment and independence to the point of isolation.

None of these traits are inherently bad.
But when they become the entire toolbox, men suffer.

Men are told to be pillars.
But pillars do not bend.
They crack.

The myth of masculinity begins early.
Little boys are encouraged to be brave, tough, loud, competitive and unfazed.
Little girls are encouraged to be nurturing, expressive, communicative and socially aware.

Boys climb.
Girls chat.
Boys wrestle.
Girls cuddle.
Boys break things.
Girls nurture things.

Not because that is what boys and girls instinctively do, but because that is what adults reward.

A boy wins approval by being fearless.
A girl wins approval by being thoughtful.

The result is a world where women grow up with emotional flexibility, and men grow up with emotional discipline.

Women know how to articulate.
Men know how to endure.

Women build community around sharing.
Men build identity around self-containment.

Then the two meet in adulthood and wonder why communication is hard.

But the real heartbreak is how men punish themselves internally. By adulthood, men have significantly fewer close friendships. Men seek psychological help at much lower rates - even when they're struggling. Across all ages, men report higher loneliness - not from lack of connection, but lack of permission to express it.

Men hide anxiety.
Men bury uncertainty.
Men protect their insecurities with bluster.
Men attach their worth to output.
Men measure themselves against fictional male archetypes.

Most men do not need to unlearn who they are.
They need to unlearn who they were told to be.

The myth of masculinity tells men they must be dominant to be confident.
But dominance is not confidence.
Dominance is insecurity wearing boots.

Confidence is grounded.
Dominance is shaky.

Confidence listens.
Dominance interrupts.
Confidence invites collaboration.
Dominance demands compliance.

Confident men are steady because they do not need to control the room.
Dominant men try to control the room because they do not feel steady.

Men are taught to confuse the two.
But women can tell the difference instantly.

A confident man makes those around him feel more relaxed.
A dominant man tightens the air.

The patriarchy rewards dominance because it looks powerful.
But within relationships, dominance is corrosive.
It blocks connection.
It blocks communication.
It blocks vulnerability.
It blocks genuine partnership.

Men who cling to dominance are not showing strength.
They are revealing how terrified they are of being seen without it.

Leadership is another part of the masculine myth that desperately needs a makeover. Men are taught that leadership means calling the shots, being the final decision-maker, and carrying themselves like a CEO. The old script insists that leadership equals control, direction, authority and decisive action delivered without hesitation and preferably with a square jaw.

But that is not leadership. That is command. And relationships are not small armies. Nobody wants to be saluted in the kitchen. Real leadership does not come from barking orders or

THE BIGGEST LIE SOLD TO MEN IS THAT **STOICISM** EQUALS **STRENGTH**.

being the one who always has an opinion locked and loaded. Real leadership in a relationship is not about deciding for someone, but creating an environment where decisions are made together without anyone needing to pull rank.

The patriarchy sold men a version of leadership that is about power rather than presence. It rewards the loudest voice, not the wisest one. It nudges men toward initiative without collaboration, which is a bit like volunteering to drive in a town you don't know, without a map, and then refusing to check if anyone else knows the directions. A man can be decisive, assertive and proactive without turning into a one-man management committee. In fact, his leadership becomes more compelling when he can pause long enough to say, "I might not have this one figured out yet; can you help?"

A man who leads without control, ego or force is rare.

Women do not want men to dominate the relationship. Contrary to some outdated online theory, no woman is lying awake at night thinking, "If only he'd micromanage me more." What women want is a man who brings steadiness without rigidity, initiative without bulldozing, and influence without pressure. Leadership without control is not weakness. It is evolution. And men who step into that version of themselves often discover that they feel lighter, freer and far more confident because they are leading from authenticity rather than expectation.

The same goes for stoicism. Stoicism is an ancient relic that men are still lugging around like an emotional boulder. Men are taught from early childhood that strength equals silence, endurance, and the ability to sit through internal chaos while maintaining the facial expression of a retired security guard. They think that being unshaken makes them strong. But rigidity is not strength. Rigidity is brittleness wearing a serious expression.

This myth trains men to reveal nothing publicly and endure everything privately, which is an excellent strategy if you are a stone monument, and a terrible strategy if you are a human being with a nervous system. The result is not heroism. The result is isolation. Men are pressured to summarise complex internal experiences in three-word sentences like "It's all good," when it is very clearly not all good. And then when they eventually reach breaking point, society looks at them with surprise, as if they spontaneously combusted out of nowhere.

Stoicism rewards silence. Silence destroys connection. Women are not impressed by stone men. They do not look at a man who never cracks, never admits hardship and never shares what is going on under the surface and think, "Wow. Incredible. A real fortress." They think, "I have absolutely no idea what is happening in there, and this is exhausting."

Women do not want men to crumble.
But they do want men who can bend.

Strength without stoicism is grounded and mature. It looks like steadiness without shutting down, honesty without panic, openness without seeing it as a confession, and the simple truth of saying, "Here's what's going on," instead of trying to win an internal battle no one else can see.

When men let go of stoicism, they do not collapse into fragility. They become three-dimensional. They discover that actual strength is flexible, responsive and human. The men who embrace this kind of strength walk through the world with a freedom they didn't know they could have. They no longer have to protect a persona. They can just be themselves.

This is where the patriarchal blueprint quietly reveals its biggest trick: it has hurt men in ways men rarely acknowledge. It has boxed them into narrow definitions that restrict their identity and compress their full humanity. Men are told that their worth is measured by performance, output, stability and control. They are scolded for softness, mocked for uncertainty, discouraged from curiosity, and trained to pretend everything is fine until pretending becomes habit.

Men often think conversations about rewriting masculinity ask them to give something up. To lose status. To lose structure. To lose identity. But rewriting masculinity is not subtraction. It is restoration. It is giving men back the parts of themselves they were told were dangerous, embarrassing or unmanly.

Men deserve the opportunity to relax.
To soften without consequence.
To ask questions without shame.
To be unsure without ridicule.
To grow at a human pace instead of a heroic one.
To speak openly without being accused of weakness.
To connect deeply without fearing they will be judged.
To change direction without being labelled inconsistent.
To need support without it being a crisis of identity.
To release pressure instead of storing it like compressed gas.
To be carried sometimes, instead of always carrying.

These are not flaws.
These are freedoms men were denied.

Rewriting masculinity does not make men less.
It makes them more.

More grounded.
More confident.
More expressive.
More steady.
More curious.
More adaptable.
More human.

These are not feminine traits.
They are universal traits.

Traits men would have naturally developed if the patriarchy had not strangled them in the crib.

The patriarchy hands men a script scribbled with rules like:
Never cry.
Never ask for help.
Never soften.
Never follow.
Never admit confusion.
Never be unsure.
Never adjust.
Never reveal the parts that make you human.

The problem is not that men *cannot* follow this script.
The problem is that they were *never meant to*.

There is nothing natural about it.
There is nothing biological about it.
It is a costume society hands out like a compulsory uniform and then applauds when men pretend it fits.

And here's the twist that explains so many of the arguments couples have: when you train a boy to avoid emotions his whole life, those emotions don't disappear - they rupture later as defensiveness, withdrawal, irritation, or panic. What looks like stubbornness is often confusion. What looks like aggression is often overwhelm. Suppression isn't emotional control. It's emotional backlog.

Men do not need to reinvent themselves.
They need to shed the regalia and reclaim the parts of themselves that masculinity once demanded they abandon. And I get it, some parts of being a bloke feel intuitive. But some might feel like they were handed to you whether you wanted them or not. Which parts feel like "you," and which feel like pressure? If you could tweak the version of masculinity you've been living with, what would you keep? What would you quietly retire?

CHAPTER TWELVE
Independence, Not Defiance
How to stand beside a strong woman without feeling pushed aside.

A few months ago, I was in a cafe meeting a couple who had booked me for their wedding. They were sweet, polite, and a little awkward, as engaged couples often are when planning one of the most significant events of their lives together. I asked all the usual pre-wedding questions. Photography style. Ceremony timing. Family politics. The vibe they wanted captured.

At one point, I turned to the bride-to-be and asked her directly, "What is most important to you on the day? What do you absolutely want photographed?"

Before she could take a breath to answer, the groom-to-be jumped in.

"Oh, we'll just go with whatever you think is best," he said confidently, as if he were offering a helpful shortcut. "We're not fussy."

I saw her face tighten. Not dramatically. Not enough for anyone else to notice. Just a tiny flicker of embarrassment, the kind that reveals itself through lowered eyes and a polite, closed-mouth smile.

I gently tried again.
"I'd love to hear from you, too," I said, keeping my attention on her.

She opened her mouth.
He answered again.

"No, seriously, we're chill. You tell us what to do, and we'll follow your lead."

She wasn't chill.
She was quiet.

Quiet because pushing back would create tension.
Quiet because having opinions made her seem difficult.
Quiet because men often expect women to be easygoing, agreeable and low maintenance, even when a wedding day is one of the few times a woman should be allowed to want things loudly.

She did not need rescuing from the decision.
She needed room to make one.

She did not need someone to translate on her behalf.
She needed her partner to stop speaking over her.

She did not need a man to streamline the process.
She needed a man who believed that her perspective mattered.

That moment was small, but it was familiar. I have seen it a hundred times. A woman quietly folding herself inward while a man confidently expands into the space that she should have been allowed to fill.

She did not lack independence.
She lacked the permission to express it.

By the time you get here, independence isn't a radical act for women anymore - it's just how life is now. But in relationships, it can stir up old fears wrapped in new packaging. This chapter isn't about history or politics. It's about the modern-day "oh shit" moments - when her independence feels like she's pulling away, when she makes decisions without checking in, when she seems fully capable without you, and you don't know what that means. Here, we look at how autonomy actually plays out between two people trying to build something together.

Independence in women is often misunderstood by men, not because women are doing anything wrong, but because, as we have already established, men were raised inside a system that taught them that their value lies in being needed.

So, when a woman says, "I can handle this," some men hear, "I do not need you."
When a woman says, "I have got it," some men hear, "You are irrelevant."
When a woman says, "I can do that myself," some men hear, "You are not useful."

The message women intend is very different.

They mean:
"I am capable."
"I respect myself."
"I trust my abilities."
"I know what I want."
"I want space to participate fully in my life."

Independence is not an attack on masculinity. It is an invitation to evolve alongside it.

Women today have grown up with opportunities their grandmothers could not imagine. Education. Financial autonomy. Career paths. Legal rights. Personal freedoms. Contraception. Divorce without social ruin. Travel. Property ownership. Entire lives designed around choice rather than survival.

They do not need men to access opportunity.
They do not need men to feel safe.
They do not need men to be financially secure.
They do not need men to feel socially validated.

They do not need men to function.

As we've already established, *need* has been replaced by *want*.

And many men were not prepared for that shift.

Because when women were dependent, men knew their role.
When women became independent, that role was redefined.

This is where the friction begins.

Some men see women's independence as a threat rather than a gift.
Some see it as resistance rather than confidence.
Some see it as disrespect rather than self-respect.
Some see it as confrontation rather than participation.

But women are not being difficult.
They are being human.

Let us look at what independence really means in a modern context.

An independent woman:
Makes decisions that reflect her values.
Sets boundaries without apologising.
Earns her own income.
Participates equally in household responsibilities.
Manages her emotional world.
Seeks mutual support, not ownership.
Speaks honestly even when it is uncomfortable.
Expects respect rather than permission.
Wants partnership, not parenthood, from her spouse.
Walks beside you, not behind or beneath you.

Independence is not the absence of vulnerability. It is the presence of self-trust.

This is why independent women make stronger partners. They are not looking for someone to save them. They are looking for someone who sees them clearly.

The tension comes from the mismatch between what men were taught and what women now expect.

Men were taught that leading equals loving.
Women now expect listening to equal loving.

Men were taught that providing equals purpose.
Women now expect emotional presence to equal purpose.

Men were taught that taking charge equals protection.
Women now expect collaboration to equal protection.

This is not because women want to emasculate men.
It is because women want connection, not hierarchy.

Women want to contribute.
Women want to participate.
Women want to build a life together rather than be slotted into a life that has been pre-designed for them.

Independence is not antagonistic. It is relational.

Many men worry that if a woman is fully independent, she might leave the relationship. They fear that independence will mean she has no reason to stay.

But independence does not make a woman more likely to leave. Lack of respect does.

Women leave relationships not because they can support themselves, but because they are tired of shrinking.
They leave because they do not feel heard.
They leave because their strength is treated as stubbornness.
They leave because their self-trust is interpreted as rebellion.

They leave because their autonomy is seen as synonymous with a threat.

Independence is not the reason women walk away.
Feeling diminished is.

And here is the irony.
When men embrace a woman's independence, she becomes more committed, not less.

Respect breeds loyalty.
Equality breeds trust.
Support breeds desire.
And when a woman feels valued for who she is, she invests deeply.

Independence strengthens relationships when men do not treat it as defiance.

A lot of men struggle with this, not because they are controlling, but because they never learned another model for masculinity. They were taught to measure their worth through action.
Open the jar.
Fix the problem.
Lift the heavy thing.
Make the decision.
Solve the conflict.
Carry the load.

They were told this is how men show love.
They were rarely told that love can also look like stepping back.
Letting her speak.
Letting her lead.
Letting her handle something because she wants to, not because you expect her to.
Letting her express preferences without getting defensive.
Letting her be autonomous without perceiving it as a threat.

Men do not lose value when they share leadership.
They gain intimacy.

Women do not pull away when they are allowed independence.
They move closer.

This is partnership, not competition.

Let us return to the bride in the cafe.

She had opinions about her wedding day.
She had preferences.
Even if she was too embarrassed to share them in front of her fiancé.

Her silence was not due to a lack of interest.
It was learned suppression.

She had likely been taught over years of small moments that speaking up made her seem demanding.
That having opinions made her difficult.
That taking up space made her inconvenient.

She would not have been defiant if she'd tried to answer my question.
She would have been independent.

But independence requires the space to express itself.
If a man keeps filling that space, her independence has nowhere to go.

Men who want strong, confident, passionate women often forget that they must make room for her strength to exist.

Relationships work best when both people get to show up as complete humans rather than assigned roles in a two-person play. You are not auditioning for "The Leader" opposite her starring role as "The Agreeable Shadow." You are building a life together where both voices matter, both needs count, and both people get to steer the ship instead of one person holding the wheel while the other quietly hopes for calm weather.

Women do not want to be managed like a project or supervised like a work experience student. They want to be met fully and honestly by someone who is not threatened by their independence. They want a partner who listens instead of assuming, collaborates instead of dictating, and understands that adulthood comes with autonomy, not a permission slip.

And here is the nice surprise: when men treat women as equal participants rather than extensions of themselves, arguments lose their sharp edges. Communication gets clearer because no one is busy contorting themselves into a version that feels safer. Respect stops being something you talk about and becomes something you naturally practice. Intimacy deepens because neither person is performing a role they did not choose.

Independence does not erase a man's usefulness. It expands the ways he can be meaningful. It shifts value away from how much weight he can carry or how decisively he can take charge, and toward how deeply he can engage, how thoughtfully he can respond, and how present he can be when his partner actually needs him. Not rescuing her. Not overriding her. Standing beside her with the quiet confidence of someone who knows partnership is not a threat.

Women never needed saving. They needed men who understood when to step in, when to step back, and when to simply stand with them. When that understanding settles into a relationship, it does not just change the dynamic; it transforms the entire atmosphere.

Everything we change in ourselves becomes the blueprint that the next generation learns from. The way we show up now - in relationships, in conversations, in conflict, in the small everyday choices - becomes the map boys inherit. And that map determines the kind of men they eventually become.

Think about a time a woman's independence rubbed you the wrong way - even if you didn't say it out loud. What story did you tell yourself about what it meant? Now flip it. What if it had nothing to do with you at all? How does that change the way you see that moment?

RELATIONSHIPS COLLAPSE WHEN **INDEPENDENCE** IS RELABELLED **INSUBORDINATION.**

CHAPTER THIRTEEN

Raising Boys (even if you're not a parent)
Small moments that shape the next generation of men.

A few weeks ago at a barbecue, one of my friend's little boys stacked it hard on the concrete path. A proper skin-scraping tumble. His eyes filled almost instantly.

Before he could react, one of the men flipping burgers shouted from across the patio, "You're fine, mate. Didn't hurt!"

It wasn't cruel.
Just... rehearsed.
The kind of line men say because it was said to them.

The kid froze.
Not because he wasn't in pain, but because he suddenly wasn't sure if he was allowed to be.

Then another of the dads walked over, crouched beside him, and said, "You copped it pretty hard, buddy. Happens to the best of us. Are you okay?"

The boy looked between them as if he wasn't sure which universe to live in.
The tough one, or the honest one.

He chose honesty.
He buried his face in the second man's chest, cried for ten seconds, then ran off laughing as if nothing had happened.

Two sentences.
Two versions of masculinity.

That is how boys learn.
Not through lectures.
Through moments.

Boys are always watching.
And men are always teaching, even when they are saying nothing at all.

We treat the raising of boys as if it is a job reserved for fathers. Something that happens behind closed doors, in households, from men who share DNA with the kids they're raising. But boys don't get shaped by genetics. They get shaped through exposure.

They learn from every man who crosses their path.
Their uncles.
Their coaches.
Their teachers.
Their mother's friends.
Their dad's friends.
Their older cousins.
Their neighbours.
The man at the barbecue who told the truth.
The man who didn't.

Boys observe masculinity long before they ever understand it.

They watch how men handle embarrassment.
They watch how men treat women.
They watch how men treat other men.
They watch what men laugh at.
They watch what men ignore.
They watch when men step up and when they step back.

And slowly, quietly, they build a blueprint for who they believe they should become.

The scary thing is:
Most men have no idea they're contributing to that blueprint because it isn't delivered in a conscious lesson. It's delivered in a moment—a fall, a joke, a correction, a silence.

Men rarely intend to shape boys this way.
But, as I've said before, intention doesn't matter.
Impact does.

Boys don't need lectures to learn the script. They absorb it through the atmosphere created by men around them.

Which means *every* man is raising boys, whether he realises it or not.

Did you know boys match girls in empathy until about age five, when socialisation begins to kick in? Research shows that adults use far fewer emotional words with boys, so of course they grow up struggling to name what they feel.

The beautiful thing is that breaking that cycle does not require perfection. Boys do not need flawless men. They need real ones. Men who are willing to course-correct, reflect, soften, listen and grow in front of them.

When a boy sees a man apologise, he learns that accountability is not humiliation.
When a boy sees a man admit he doesn't know something, he learns that uncertainty is not weakness.
When a boy sees a man speak respectfully to women, he learns that respect is the baseline, not a bonus.
When a boy sees a man stay calm instead of exploding, he learns that strength is steady, not loud.
When a boy sees a man comfort someone, he learns that care is not gendered.

None of these moments require parenting.
They require presence.

A boy who sees a man change his behaviour learns that masculinity evolves.
A boy who sees a man listen learns that masculinity includes humility.
A boy who sees a man ask for help learns that masculinity is collaborative.
A boy who sees a man treat him gently after a fall learns that masculinity makes room for pain.

This is how boys learn to be better men without anyone sitting them down for a talk.

They learn by watching men choose differently.

Boys are constantly measuring themselves against the men they see.
Not because they lack identity, but because identity is built from exposure.

Show them that anger is the only acceptable reaction, and they will grow into men who treat it as a toolkit.
Show them humour as a weapon, and they will grow into men who use sarcasm to wound.
Show them dominance, and they will grow into men who think control equals partnership.
Show them indifference, and they will grow into men who shut down instead of leaning in.

But show them boundaries that include compassion, kindness and structure?
They grow into balanced men.

Boys don't need perfect masculinity.
They need practised masculinity.

One of the most powerful things a man can do for the next generation is challenge the parts of the script he inherited but no longer wants.

Men often underestimate the impact of the tiny corrections.
The gentle rewrites.
The quiet "Hang on, mate, that's not how we do things anymore."

A boy hears two men disagreeing about how pain should be handled.
He learns that there is more than one way to be male.

A boy hears a man say, "It's okay to be upset."
He learns that emotional honesty is not forbidden territory.

A boy hears a man make space for him.
He learns adulthood does not require shrinking himself.

A boy hears a man refuse to laugh at a sexist joke.
He learns respect outranks conformity.

These are moments men dismiss as small.
But boys use them as a compass.

Most boys do not want to be the loudest, the strongest, or the most dominant.
They want to be accepted.
They want to know they are allowed to be human.

And the only way to teach that is by modelling humanity in front of them.

One of the biggest misconceptions adult men have is that boys listen most to the charismatic, confident, attention-grabbing men. They don't.

Boys listen most to the men who see them.

The man who kneels to their level.
The man who answers their questions instead of brushing them off.

'TOUGHEN UP' DOESN'T BUILD RESILIENCE. IT BUILDS REPRESSION AND DYSREGULATION.

The man who doesn't mock them when they hesitate.
The man who treats their thoughts seriously.
The man who takes an interest in what they care about.
The man who respects their pace instead of rushing them.
The man who corrects them without humiliating them.
The man who makes eye contact when talking to them.
The man who notices when they're unsure.

You do not need to be a father to be that man.
You need to show up in the moments when boys are quietly taking notes.

Even teenage boys, with their bravado and loudness, still notice which men deserve respect. They pay attention to the men who have nothing to prove. They pay attention to the men who don't need to shout to be heard. They pay attention to the men who can laugh without being cruel.

Boys gravitate toward men who feel safe.

And *safe* does not mean *soft*.
Safe means grounded.

Influencing boys also includes the things men choose not to let slide. Sometimes raising better boys is not about the behaviour you model, but about the behaviour you interrupt.

A boy watches a man say nothing when someone makes a cruel joke.
He learns silence is consent.

A boy watches a man shake his head and say, "Come on, mate, not that," when someone crosses the line.
He learns lines *exist*.

A boy watches a man gently correct a peer.
He learns courage can be quiet.

A boy watches a man refuse to cheer for aggression.
He learns that strength is not violence.

A boy watches a man show kindness in a moment where being dismissive would be easier.
He learns that kindness is masculine, too.

These are not dramatic events.
They are micro-adjustments in the environment in which boys grow up.

Men do not need to be heroes.
They need to avoid becoming the men who perpetuate a system that damages boys without realising it.

Another important truth:
Boys learn how to treat women by watching how men treat women.

If a man jokes about women loudly, a boy learns that mocking women is socially rewarding.
If a man treats women with respect and equality, a boy learns that respect is the norm.
If a man listens to a woman speak without interrupting, the boy learns that women are worth listening to.
If a man blames women for his frustration, the boy learns that blaming is acceptable.
If a man takes responsibility without excuses, the boy learns that accountability is masculine.

Men underestimate how deeply boys internalise male behaviour around women.

Boys can smell hypocrisy.
They can hear double standards.
They can sense when a man is putting on a show.
They can tell who actually respects women and who pays lip service to respect when it looks good.

If men truly want better boys, they must model the version of masculinity they want replicated.

You cannot teach respect while practising entitlement.
You cannot teach humility while practising defensiveness.
You cannot teach empathy while practising dismissiveness.

Boys learn by imitation.

Give them something *worth imitating*.

You don't need credentials to influence boys. You don't need children. You don't need a teaching degree, or a psychological background, or any special expertise.

All you need is the willingness to be aware of your impact.
All you need is the consciousness to pause before reinforcing the script you inherited.
All you need is the willingness to model a version of masculinity that chips away at the silent rules boys still absorb every day.

Men shape boyhood through presence.
And every boy, whether or not he says it out loud, is looking for clues about how to become a man.

Show him that strength is steady.
Show him that respect is the default.
Show him that compassion is masculine.
Show him that confidence is quiet.
Show him that accountability is noble.
Show him that gentleness is allowed.
Show him that no man is diminished by kindness.
Show him that manhood evolves.

Because every boy grows into a man who remembers the men he watched most closely.
And your influence, whether or not you realise it, is part of that memory.

Think of the younger blokes around you - teens, apprentices, nephews, the lads at work. They notice how you talk, how you joke, how you treat women, how you handle stress. If one of them copied your behaviour word-for-word, would you be proud of the result?

CHAPTER FOURTEEN
A Little Nudge, a Big Impact
When small shifts in behaviour create significant changes for the women around you.

A friend of mine told me about a moment at work that sounded small at first, but was actually a very clear example of allyship.

She had been presenting in a meeting. Running through updates, sharing outcomes, answering questions. This was not a new environment for her—she was often responsible for running large-scale discussions and providing feedback to her team.

Halfway through explaining a point, one man in the room cut her off.
Not aggressively.
Not with malice.
Just casually.
The way men often interrupt women without realising they are doing it.

He talked over the top of her.
He expanded on her point as though it were his.
He gestured like he was now in charge of the conversation.

She went quiet. Not because she didn't know what to say, but because she'd been here before. The moment was familiar. Predictable. Exhausting.

Then something different happened.

Another man in the meeting leaned slightly forward, raised a hand and said, "Hang on. I want to hear the rest of what she was saying."

Simple.
Calm.
No grand speeches about equality.
No theatrics.
No applause.

Just a sentence.

The room shifted.
The original interrupter stopped talking.
She had the floor again.
She finished her point.
The meeting moved on.

Afterwards, she told me how refreshing it felt to have a man actually notice those dynamics at play. Not because she needed rescuing, but because someone restored the space that was already hers. Someone saw the imbalance and nudged it back into alignment.

That is allyship.
Not the big, dramatic gestures.
The small, deliberate ones.

When men hear the word "ally," they sometimes imagine they need to become loud activists or professional feminists who quote statistics at barbecues. They picture having to jump into every conversation with a megaphone and a moral lesson. It feels heavy. Performative. Like a job description they didn't apply for.

But allyship is not a role.
It is a posture.

It is how a man stands in moments where he has influence he may not even realise he holds.

It is steady, not loud.
Supportive, not patronising.
Consistent, not theatrical.

Women do not expect men to become full-time defenders or knights in shining armour. In fact, most women do not want men to swoop in dramatically at all. They want something much simpler.

They want men who make the world slightly less exhausting for them.
Men who reduce friction instead of creating it.
Men who use their influence to rebalance the room, not dominate it.
Men who notice the dynamics women are constantly forced to navigate.

Allyship, in everyday life, is not heroic.
It is human.

Many men genuinely want to be allies, but they overthink it. They imagine they need advanced scripts or perfectly crafted interventions. They worry about saying the wrong thing, or that they will look patronising, or that other men will judge them.

And because they overthink it, they do nothing.

But allyship is not about eloquence.
It is about presence.
It is about the micro-decisions men make each day that ripple outward.

For example, a man who notices a woman being spoken over and saying, "I think she was still speaking," is demonstrating allyship. Studies show women get interrupted up to three times more than men in mixed-gender conversations. So, the moment you speak up? She feels it immediately.

A man who stops a joke from becoming a pile-on by saying, "Alright, leave it," is demonstrating allyship.

A man who does not laugh at a misogynistic joke and instead gives a quiet, unimpressed look is demonstrating allyship.

A man who shares the mental load in meetings instead of letting women run all the admin and organisation is demonstrating allyship.

A man who checks in with a colleague after someone spoke to her sharply is demonstrating allyship.

A man who steps aside in conversation so women don't have to fight for oxygen is demonstrating allyship.

None of this requires speeches.
It requires awareness.
And awareness is free.

Women navigate hundreds of power imbalances each year that men never experience.
Not because men are privileged villains, but because the world is built on patterns men rarely notice.

Allyship begins when men *start noticing*.

Noticing when women shrink because they are interrupted.
Noticing when women soften their tone because a man has escalated.
Noticing when women apologise for taking up space.
Noticing when women are ignored after making a point.
Noticing when women are assigned emotional labour by default.
Noticing when women laugh politely at jokes that are not funny, because disagreeing might cause tension.

Men often say, "I had no idea that happened so much."

That sentence isn't shameful.
It is the beginning.

Because once a man knows, inaction becomes a decision.

Not with aggression.
Not with dominance.
With subtlety.

Subtlety is the backbone of everyday allyship.

Some men think allyship means confronting other men aggressively.
It doesn't.
That usually makes everything worse.

The goal is not to become a moral enforcer.
The goal is to shift the atmosphere with small, steady corrections.

Women do not need men to start fights.
They need men to stop patterns.

For example:
In a meeting, if a woman is interrupted, an ally does not bark, "Stop talking over her."
He simply says, "Let's hear her out."

If a man makes a sexist joke, an ally does not turn it into a confrontation.
He gives a flat, unimpressed "Really?" and changes the subject.
Social discomfort does the rest.

If a woman is talked down to, an ally does not escalate tension.
He says, "She already explained that," or "She knows this area well."

Allyship is rarely a performance.

IF YOU CAN SPEAK OVER A WOMAN, YOU CAN CERTAINLY SPEAK UP FOR ONE.

It is almost always a correction in tone.

It protects the dignity of everyone involved while still shifting the dynamic.

Another overlooked form of allyship is redirecting social attention to reduce pressure on women. Women spend a lot of time managing how they are perceived. Men can help simply by creating space for women to exist without having to perform.

For example, when a woman is shy in a group, an ally does not put her on the spot.
He creates gentle pauses where she can speak if she chooses.

When a woman is being cornered in conversation, an ally does not swoop in theatrically.
He interrupts casually with a question or a distraction that gives her an exit.

When a woman is being talked at relentlessly, an ally redirects the conversation to include her preferences rather than turning her into an audience.

When a woman seems uncomfortable with a comment, an ally pivots the conversation without making her defend herself.

These actions do not draw attention to her.
They remove the pressure from her.

Allyship is rarely glamorous.
It is graceful.

Allyship means managing other men without humiliating them.
Men shut down when they are embarrassed.
They open up when they are guided.

If a man is talking too loudly, an ally lowers his own voice.
The room follows.

If a man is taking up too much space, an ally shifts the dynamic by turning attention toward someone else.

If a man is making a joke that leans on sexist tropes, an ally doesn't give it oxygen.
Starving a joke of laughter kills it faster than confrontation ever could.

If a man is dominating a conversation, an ally says, "Hang on, I want to hear what she was saying," instead of "Stop talking."
The first preserves dignity.
The second invites defensiveness.

These are small behaviours.
But they build trust.
They say, "I see what's happening. And I'm using my position to level the field."

Women do not want protectors.
They want partners.
Partnering is active, not passive.

And boys watching nearby learn which approach builds the better man.

Allyship is also internal.
It's not just what men do externally.
It's what they examine within themselves.

Men raised in a patriarchal world inherit habits they didn't choose.
Allyship means noticing them.

It means realising when your first instinct is to speak instead of listen.
It means catching the subtle urge to explain something she already knows.
It means questioning the reflexive belief that you are right.

It means pausing before correcting tone, rather than focusing on the content.
It means recognising when you are defending your ego instead of the point.
It means interrogating the urge to be the centre of attention instead of sharing the space.

Internal allyship is the version nobody sees, but women feel.

It is the kind of allyship that strengthens relationships by removing the micro-frictions that chip away at trust.

Men who practice internal allyship become easier to talk to, easier to trust, easier to collaborate with, and easier to love.

Women respond not to perfection but to presence.

And presence grows when ego stops taking up all the space.

Women do not need grand gestures.
They need men who choose better, moment by moment.

Look back over the past week. What was one moment you could've stepped up, said something, or picked up a task before being asked - but didn't? What stopped you? What small thing could you do differently next time?

CHAPTER FIFTEEN
The Antidote
Where the work begins.

A few months ago, I was having a long, meandering debate with a male friend about the so-called "natural roles" of men and women. The kind of back and forth you have with someone smart who genuinely wants to understand other perspectives, but has spent most of his life hearing one story about how the world supposedly works.

We were talking about the mental load. I explained that women aren't naturally better at remembering birthdays, anticipating needs, or keeping track of schedules, and that none of that is instinct; it is societal expectation. He pushed back at first with the usual lines men fall back on, the ones they don't even realise they absorbed along the way.

"But women just... notice things more," he said.
"Women are more organised."
"Women multitask better."

I told him those things weren't biology. They were practised. Repeated. Normalized. The invisible curriculum women get handed before they can even articulate what it is they are learning. I also gave the example of men at work—entirely capable of showing initiative, making lists, remembering (and executing) tasks. They are the same skills, just exhibited in a different environment, one in which they are noticed and rewarded.

He was quiet for a moment. Then he cocked his head slightly, as if something had shifted just a couple of degrees to the left, and said, "Yeah... ok. I hadn't thought of it like that."

He didn't say it defensively or resentfully.
He said it like someone realising a door had been open the whole time, and he had simply never noticed.

It wasn't a transformation.
It was an adjustment.
A pivot.
A shift in awareness.

And that's the real point.
Change doesn't start with a revolution.
It starts with a head tilt and "I hadn't thought of it like that."

That tiny moment stuck with me. Not because it was a fireworks moment with inspirational violins swelling dramatically in the background. But because it wasn't. It was just a man realising a blind spot he didn't know he had. He didn't get defensive. He didn't spiral into shame. He simply… updated himself like a phone that finally stopped ignoring the software notification.

That moment wasn't about romance. It wasn't about a partner or a spouse. It was about how he moved through the world with every woman in his life. His mum. His sister. His female colleagues. His friends. His future daughter, if he ever had one. A slight shift in his understanding of things translated instantly and seamlessly into how he treated them all.

And honestly, that is what women are asking for. Not dramatic reinvention. Not emotional gymnastics. Just updates. The small kind. The "huh, fair point" kind. The kind where a man tweaks his perspective the way he tweaks the settings on a new TV until the colours look right.

Women don't want men to throw out the whole operating system.
They want men to stop pretending the glitches are features.

The funny thing is that men are excellent at updating almost everything else. A man will spend 14 hours researching the best lawn mower, but act like understanding why his partner is irritated is rocket science. A man will learn the rules of a sport he discovered two minutes ago, but apparently, learning what mental load is requires a PhD and a research grant.

But women know the truth.
Men are smart.
Men are capable.
Men can learn anything when they decide it matters.

And that right there is the key to this entire book. You deciding it matters. You deciding *we* matter.

The way you show up for women is not confined to romantic relationships. The same behaviors that strengthen a marriage also strengthen a friendship. The same habits that build safety for a partner also build safety for a daughter. The same presence that softens conflict at home also softens misunderstandings at work. The same awareness that reduces the burden on a wife also reduces the burden on a mother who has spent her entire life carrying more than she should have.

Men's impact is never limited to one woman.
It ripples outward to every woman they interact with.

Women feel it everywhere.
In their relationship with their dad.
In the way male teachers engage them in the classroom.
In the way boys talk to them at school.
In the way male friends treat them at eighteen.
In the way male colleagues treat them at thirty.
In the way sons speak to their mothers.
In the way men speak about women when they think no women are around.

We often pretend romantic relationships are at the centre of gender dynamics. They're not. They're just the most obvious place they play out. Everything men learn about understanding, responding to, and relating to women starts long before they ever hold someone's hand.

This is what people mean when they say men can be part of the solution.
It is not about theory. It is about the impact men have in the daily orbit of women's lives.

Every woman has a story about a man who changed the atmosphere simply by choosing to be present instead of defensive. Most women can also tell you about a man who made everything harder by doing the opposite.

The difference between the two men is rarely personality.
It is awareness.
It is purpose.
It is the choice to participate rather than react.

And the good news is that choice is available to every man, regardless of age, background or temperament.

If you've read this far, you already know the pressure points women navigate. You know that women carry invisible layers of effort that men don't always see. You know the mental load isn't a myth, but a lived reality. You know emotional safety isn't about coddling but about creating stability. You know women are not inherently better at domestic logistics, but socially conditioned into doing them.

And hopefully, you know this: none of these truths require men to feel guilty.
Just aware.

Awareness is the beginning of everything.
Awareness is what turns a good man into a deeply impactful one.

Awareness is what transforms "I didn't know" into "I can do better now that I do."

Women are not asking for apologies for the past.
They are asking for attention in the present.

Attention to tone.
Attention to reaction.
Attention to load.
Attention to behaviour.
Attention to impact.

The point of this book has never been to dictate what masculinity should be. It has been to hold up a mirror to the parts of masculinity that are workable and the parts that are simply habitual. The parts that are human and the parts that are inherited. The parts that lift women and the parts that exhaust them.

Men are not broken.
Masculinity is not broken.
But the autopilot version of both needs updating.

The impacts of those updates are universal.

Because the women in men's lives are not separate categories.
They are interconnected circles.
The way men treat one influences how others experience them.

You cannot be dismissive of your partner and then curious with your daughter.
You cannot belittle your sister and then tell your female friends you respect women.
You cannot treat your mum as the family workhorse and then treat your partner like an equal.
You cannot make female colleagues uncomfortable and then insist you're a good man at home.

Women feel the whole picture.
Not the curated pockets of it.

Men who want meaningful relationships with the women in their lives must bring consistency across the board.

Not *perfection*.
Consistency.

Your shift does not need to be dramatic. It doesn't need to be theatrical, polished, or perfect. It can be as small as noticing something you didn't notice before. A pause instead of a reflex. A question instead of a defence. A moment where you stop and think, "What is actually happening here?" rather than letting old habits run the show.

Because when men shift even slightly, it creates space. Not the delicate, airy kind of space people talk about on self-help posters. Real space. The kind that lets women move through the world without having to work twice as hard just to be heard, respected, or safe. The type that reduces the background noise women live with every day, because the system is set up to treat them as secondary unless someone intentionally chooses otherwise.

Women do not need gentleness for the sake of being gentle.
They need equality.
They need access.
They need safety.
They need to participate fully without being sidelined, minimised or doubted.

And men, whether they realise it or not, have a daily influence on those conditions. Not because men are controlling villains, but because the system was built in their favour. So, when a man chooses to see the system instead of pretending it isn't there, the ground shifts. Even if only slightly. And that slight shift can change the way an entire interaction unfolds.

Women are not asking men to treat them like fragile things that need calm atmospheres or emotional cushioning. They are asking men to recognise the dynamics they walk through - the interruptions, the disbelief, the assumptions, the everyday silencing - and not participate in them. To notice when the system tries to speak for them or over them, and decide not to join that chorus.

The ways you show up matter because they can either reinforce the system or disrupt it.

And that choice is what women feel most. Not softness. Not protection. Not special treatment. What they feel is whether a man is standing with them inside the reality they navigate, or whether he is floating above it, assuming everything is fine because it feels fine to *him*.

Your presence can make a conversation safer, not because she is fragile, but because the world has taught her what happens when she speaks up.
Your tone can make room for her voice, not because she needs permission, but because men's voices are still the ones positioned as default.
Your awareness can ease the burden she carries, not because she is overwhelmed, but because she has been overburdened by cultural design, not personal weakness.

This isn't about calmness.
It's about fairness.
It's about access.
It's about agency.

And when men choose to show up with awareness, everything becomes more possible for the women around them. Women are not asking men to cushion them. They are asking men to stop adding weight where the world already piles it on.

If you love us - *any* of us - let that love be visible in how you

participate.
Not because we are delicate.
But because the world we move through is uneven.
And you are in a position to help level it.

Most discussions about allyship focus on how it helps women, which matters deeply. But there's another part of the story - one men rarely hear.

Being an ally doesn't just make the world safer for women.
It makes *your* world bigger, richer, and less lonely.

When a man steps in to interrupt a harmful comment, or backs a woman's idea in a meeting, or refuses to laugh along with something he knows isn't right, he isn't only supporting her. He's quietly freeing himself from the pressure to perform a version of masculinity that never actually fit him.

Allyship permits men to be more than the script they were handed.

It builds deeper friendships because other good men recognise you instantly.
It builds trust with the women in your life because they no longer have to calculate their safety around you.
It lowers the pressure to be the "strong one" all the time, because strength stops being about dominance and becomes about integrity.
It gives you relationships - romantic, social, professional - that are grounded in honesty instead of performance.

And the funny thing is: men who show up for women consistently find that other men feel safer showing up for them.

Allyship isn't self-sacrifice.
It's self-expansion.

If you've made it this far, something in you already wants to be better - not because you're broken, not because you're the villain, but because you finally understand the impact you have.

That's the real epiphany here: ***you matter.***
Your choices matter.
Your silence matters.
Your attitude, your reactions, your presence - they shape the world women walk through every single day.

Walk out of this book aware of your influence.
Walk out paying attention.
Walk out determined to leave women feeling safer, stronger, and more seen than before you opened the first page.

And if you can manage all that *without* circling back later asking, "Did you see what I did there?" — because you've realised the point isn't credit, it's impact - well... that's a crisp high-five moment. It means something in these pages landed exactly where it needed to.

We've travelled through this uneven house together, room by room. We've looked at the foundations, the tilt, the quiet patterns you were never taught to see. And now the real work begins, where the book ends: in how you move through the world now that you can feel the floor beneath your feet.

www.ingramcontent.com/pod-product-compliance
Lightning Source LLC
Chambersburg PA
CBHW071714020426
42333CB00017B/2258